Discover Martha's Vineyard

AMC's Guide to the Best Hiking, Biking, and Paddling

LEE SINAI

Illustrated by
JOYCE S. SHERR

Appalachian Mountain Club Books
Boston, Massachusetts

The AMC is a nonprofit organization and sales of AMC books fund our mission of protecting the Northeast outdoors. If you appreciate our efforts and would like to make a donation to the AMC, contact us at Appalachian Mountain Club, 5 Joy Street, Boston, MA 02108.

http://www.outdoors.org/publications/books

Distributed by the Globe Pequot Press, Guilford, Connecticut.

Front cover photographs (l-r): © BrightQube, © Masterfile, © BrightQube, © iStock
Back cover photographs (l-r): © BrightQube, © Sojourn Bicycling and Active Vacations/GoSojourn.com, © Lee Sinai
Book design by Eric Edstam
Maps by Ken Dumas, © AMC
Illustrations © Joyce Sherr
All interior photographs © Lee Sinai except for those on pages: i © Joy Marzolf; xvii, 9, 37, 177 © Paul Rezendes; 109, 157 © Sojourn Bicycling and Active Vacations/GoSojourn.com; 146 © iStock; 189 © Jerry and Marcy Monkman/Ecophotography.com

Library of Congress Cataloging-in-Publication Data
Sinai, Lee.
  Discover Martha's Vineyard : AMC's guide to the best hiking, biking, and paddling / by Lee Sinai.
    p. cm.
  Includes index.
  ISBN 978-1-934028-24-7
1. Bicycle touring—Massachusetts—Martha's Vineyard—Guidebooks. 2. Hiking—Massachusetts—Martha's Vineyard—Guidebooks. 3. Kayaking—Massachusetts—Martha's Vineyard—Guidebooks. 4. Martha's Vineyard (Mass.)—Guidebooks. I. Appalachian Mountain Club. II. Title.
  GV1045.5.M42M377 2009
  917.44'94—dc22
                    2009000320

The paper used in this publication meets the minimum requirements of the American National Standard for Information Sciences-Permanence of Paper for Printed Library Materials, ANSI Z39.48-1984. ∞

Outdoor recreation activities by their very nature are potentially hazardous. This book is not a substitute for good personal judgment and training in outdoor skills. Due to changes in conditions, use of the information in this book is at the sole risk of the user. The author and the Appalachian Mountain Club assume no liability for accidents happening to, or injuries sustained by, readers who engage in the activities described in this book.

Printed in the United States of America.

Printed on paper that contains 30 percent post-consumer recycled fiber, using soy-based inks.

10 9 8 7 6 5 4 3 2 1   09 10 11 12 13 14 15 16

Locator Map

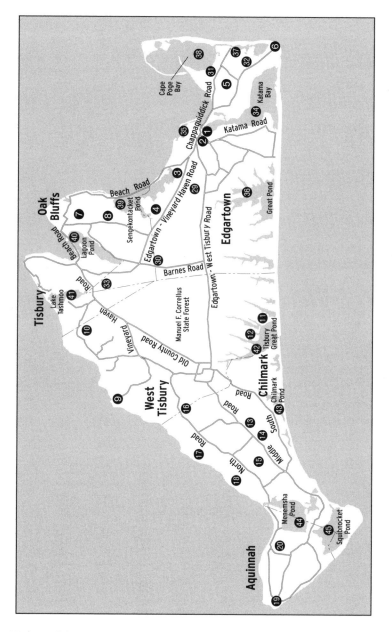

Trips 21 through 28 are not marked on map because these on-road biking trips span a large portion of Martha's Vineyard.

Contents

AT-A-GLANCE TRIP PLANNER

#	Trip	Page	Location (Town)	Distance	Rating
	WALKING AND HIKING				
1	Edgartown and Lighthouse Beach	1	Edgartown	3.4 mi	Easy
2	Sheriff's Meadow Sanctuary	12	Edgartown	0.5 mi	Easy
3	Caroline Tuthill Wildlife Preserve	17	Edgartown	1.4 mi	Easy
4	Felix Neck Wildlife Sanctuary	22	Edgartown	1.5 mi	Easy
5	Mytoi Garden-East Beach	27	Chappaquiddick	1.0 mi	Easy
6	Wasque Reservation	33	Chappaquiddick	3.0 mi	Easy
7	Camp Meeting Grounds	38	Oak Bluffs	1.3 mi	Easy
8	Trade Wind Fields Preserve	45	Oak Bluffs	1.3–3.0 mi	Easy
9	Cedar Tree Neck Wildlife Sanctuary	49	West Tisbury	2.8 mi	Moderate
10	Blackwater Pond Reservation and Wompesket Preserve	54	West Tisbury	3.5 mi	Easy
11	Long Point Wildlife Refuge	59	West Tisbury	3.0 mi	Easy

Good for Kids	Dogs Allowed	Fees	Swimming	Trip Highlights
🚶	🐕	$	🏊	Sightseeing and swimming; biking permitted; universal access
🚶				Short and shaded
🚶	🐕			Tranquil, convenient, scenic
🚶		$		Nature walk with plentiful wildlife; universal access
🚶		$	🏊	Arboretum and 4-star beach; universal access
🚶	🐕	$	🏊	Great swimming, birding, and biking; universal access
🚶		$	🏊	Historic tour
🚶	🐕			Premiere dog-walker's destination; also good for biking; universal access
🚶	🐕			Dazzling views from a variety of ecosystems
🚶	🐕			Enjoyable hiking through diverse terrain; biking permitted; universal access
🚶	🐕	$	🏊	Ocean, ponds, trails; biking permitted

Good for Kids	Dogs Allowed	Fees	Swimming	Trip Highlights
🚶	🐕		🏊	Terrific hot-weather hike; biking permitted
🚶	🐕		🏊	Tranquil hike
🚶	🐕			Hike beside the Fulling Mill Brook; biking permitted
🚶	🐕			Climb for panoramas; biking permitted; universal access
🚶	🐕			Hike or bike to the rock
🚶	🐕		🏊	Short stroll to a pristine beach; biking permitted; universal access
				Outstanding views, varied topography; universal access
		$	🏊	A must see; universal access
🚶	🐕			Short and sweet; biking permitted; universal access
🚶			🏊	Three-town tour, seascapes
🚶		$	🏊	Smaller island tour
🚶			🏊	Panoramic beach ride
🚶			🏊	Historic, scenic ride
🚶		$	🏊	Farms and forest
				Short and picturesque
			🏊	Hills, views, fishing village
				Longest ride, panoramic views

Good for Kids	Dogs Allowed	Fees	Swimming	Trip Highlights
	🐕			Ancient ways link with new trails; universal access
	🐕			Wide variety of terrain; universal access
	🐕	$	🏊	Chappy off-road; universal access
🚶	🐕			Short, salt marsh; universal access
	🐕			Mellow to challenging; universal access
			🏊	Busy bay and tranquil pond
			🏊	Mansions and yachts
			🏊	Scenic, protected coves
		$	🏊	Ideal for inexperienced paddlers and bird watchers
		$	🏊	Remote paddling in a pristine bay
			🏊	Lots to see and do
			🏊	Conveniently located near kayak rentals
			🏊	Small, scenic
			🏊	Coves, inlets, ponds
			🏊	Variety and tranquility
			🏊	Three interconnected ponds
			🏊	Bucolic and beautiful

Acknowledgments

I AM GRATEFUL TO MANY PEOPLE for their contributions to this book. My family, especially, deserves heartfelt thanks. Allen, Lauren, and Todd have been so encouraging and tremendously helpful.

I am most appreciative of the time and information accorded me by James Lengyel, director, and Matthew Dix, land superintendent, of the Martha's Vineyard Land Bank, Kristen Fauteux, director of stewardship for the Sheriff's Meadow Foundation; John Varkonda, superintendent of the Manuel F. Corellus State Forest; Bill Veno, senior planner at the Martha's Vineyard Commission; Chris Kennedy, director of The Trustees of Reservations; and Suzan Bellincampi, director of Felix Neck Wildlife Sanctuary.

Professor George Ellmore of Tufts University willingly shared his botanical knowledge as did Lindsay Allison, who walked around Mytoi with me. I am so appreciative of my friends who read and commented on the trips, tested bike rides and hikes, and were always supportive. Special thanks to Rhoda Fischer, Barbara and Don McLagan, and Joyce Sherr, the illustrator, who also provided information and helpful advice.

Stewardship and Conservation

The Appalachian Mountain Club (AMC) is a national educational partner of Leave No Trace, Inc, a nonprofit organization dedicated to promoting and inspiring responsible outdoor recreation through education, research, and partnerships. The Leave No Trace program seeks to develop wildland ethics—ways in which you can act in the outdoors to minimize your impact on the areas you visit and to protect our natural resources for future enjoyment. Leave No Trace unites four federal land management agencies—the U.S. Forest Service, National Park Service, Bureau of Land Management, and U.S. Fish and Wildlife Service—with manufacturers, outdoor retailers, user groups, educators, organizations such as the AMC and the National Outdoor Leadership School (NOLS), and individuals.

The Leave No Trace ethic is guided by these seven principles:
- Plan ahead and prepare.
- Travel and camp on durable surfaces.
- Dispose of waste properly.
- Leave what you find.
- Minimize campfire impacts.
- Respect wildlife.
- Be considerate of other visitors.

The AMC has joined NOLS—a recognized leader in wilderness education and a founding partner of Leave No Trace—as a national provider of the Leave No Trace Master Educator Course. The AMC offers this five-day course, designed especially for outdoor professionals and land managers, as well as the shorter two-day Leave No Trace Trainer course, at locations throughout the Northeast.

For Leave No Trace information and materials, contact:

Leave No Trace Center for Outdoor Ethics, P.O. Box 997, Boulder, CO, 80306

Toll Free: 800-332-4100: Fax: 303-442-8217

www.lnt.org.

Introduction to Martha's Vineyard

WHY HAS MARTHA'S VINEYARD CONTINUED TO RETAIN its unique appeal? One reason for its popularity and a key to Martha's Vineyard's allure is its large number of scenic unspoiled areas. Far-sighted philanthropists and aggressive land conservation have allowed much of the Vineyard to remain as it was centuries ago. Once you step off the ferry or airplane and head out of the town centers, you feel as if you truly have escaped from the mainland. Tranquil sanctuaries, picturesque ponds, and miles of bike paths encourage a "get-away-from-it-all" experience. But locating these often obscure spots can be a real challenge. In this book, I tell you how to find these places and then guide you through them on foot, on bike, and in your canoe or kayak, while pointing out their history and unique natural features. *Discover Martha's Vineyard* serves as a comprehensive guide to the Vineyard, since it describes the island's major attractions as well as its hidden treasures.

For an island with six decidedly different towns and a wide variety of natural resources, Martha's Vineyard is surprisingly compact, stretching just 23 miles from the Gay Head Cliffs at its western end to the Chappaquiddick beaches at its eastern end. Because the island is small and has fairly level terrain, it's an ideal place to bike and hike. With recent additions, the island can now boast 37 miles of bike paths that allow for a relaxing exploration without worries about traffic, parking, and speed limits.

Martha's Vineyard is famous for miles of sandy beaches and scenic coastline, but its other less well-known but equally picturesque assets are its large ponds and bays, often rimmed by long thin coves. The best way to explore these bodies of water is by canoe or kayak. Paddling encourages a leisurely exploration and allows for the flexibility to stop and swim at remote beaches or hike on conservation land. In this book, you'll discover twelve bodies of water that permit public access and have designated spots for parking your car and unloading your watercraft.

Climate

The best months to visit Martha's Vineyard are September and June, when the island is less crowded and the temperature and humidity are lower. The busiest and most humid month is August. Also warm but not quite so busy is July, except for the July 4th week, the busiest of the summer. October and May tend to be cooler and rainier but with fewer tourists and less expensive accommodations.

AVERAGE TEMPERATURES AND RAINFALL

Month	High	Low	Inches
April	54	38	4.25
May	64	47	3.55
June	73	56	3.51
July	79	62	3.10
August	78	62	3.96
September	72	56	3.48
October	62	45	3.95

Getting to the Vineyard

If you are arriving on Martha's Vineyard by ferry, you can bring your bicycle for a modest extra charge. If you drive onto the ferry, you do not have to pay a fee for your bicycle. Ferries to Martha's Vineyard leave from New Bedford, Hyannis, Falmouth, Woods Hole, and North Kingston, R.I. The Express Ferry from New Bedford (866-683-3779; www.mvexpressferry.com) takes one hour and makes seven to ten round-trips daily in summer. The Hy-Line (800-492-8082; www.hylinecruises.com) runs both a high-speed ferry and traditional ferry from Hyannis. The high-speed ferry takes half the time (one hour), runs five times a day (as opposed to once a day for the traditional ferry), and is double the price. The Island Queen (508-548-4800; www.islandqueen.com) leaves from Falmouth Harbor seven to nine times a day, is less expensive and takes only 35 minutes. These ferries only run from Memorial Day to Columbus Day, disembark in Oak Bluffs, and do not carry cars.

The Falmouth Ferry Service (508-548-9400; www.falmouthferry.com) runs from Falmouth to Edgartown and takes one hour. It runs six times a day

Martha's Vineyard Steamship Authority Ferry in Vineyard Haven Harbor.

in summer and four times a day in spring and fall. The Woods Hole, Martha's Vineyard and Nantucket Steamship Authority boats (508-477-8600; www.steamshipauthority.com) are larger, carry cars, and run year-round. The trip takes 45 minutes and disembarks in both Vineyard Haven and Oak Bluffs. However, parking in Woods Hole can be a problem. In Falmouth, there is a parking lot next to the Island Queen. In Woods Hole, passengers must ride a shuttle bus or bike from the parking lot to the ferry dock. The 3.25-mile Shining Sea Bikeway, located 0.25 mile to the right of Palmer Street Parking, leads to the Steamship Authority Dock in Woods Hole.

If you arrive on the Vineyard by plane, you can hail a cab or ride a shuttle bus to your lodgings and rent a bike at one of the bike rental shops listed in the appendix.

Island-Wide Transportation

Martha's Vineyard prides itself on its excellent transportation system. The Martha's Vineyard Transit Authority (508-693-9440; www.vineyardtransit.com) runs buses all over the island with frequent, inexpensive trips among all the towns and from the ferries and airport. Many of the buses are fitted with bike racks so if one tires of pedaling, you can hop on a bus.

Lodging

Many hotels, inns, and bed-and-breakfasts are located all over the island. The Martha's Vineyard Chamber of Commerce (800-505-4815; www.mvy.com) can assist you in finding accommodations.

In addition, there is a campground and a hostel. The Martha's Vineyard Family Campground (508-693-3772; www.campmvfc.com), open from May 23 to October 15, is situated 0.5 mile from Vineyard Haven Center at 569 Edgartown Road. Hostelling International (508-693-2665; www.usahostels.org), open from May 16 to October 13, abuts the bike path in the Manuel Corellus State Forest in West Tisbury.

Food

Fast, slow, inexpensive, and pricey meals are all over the island. What you won't find are chain restaurants, as they are prohibited, except for Dairy Queen, which was on the island before the ruling was passed. Oak Bluffs has more inexpensive and fast-food restaurants than other towns, while Edgartown boasts the fancier places.

Fees

Most of the reservations and preserves are free, with the exception of Felix Neck Wildlife Sanctuary and two of The Trustees of Reservations beaches: Long Point Wildlife Refuge and Wasque Reservation.

Universal Access

The Martha's Vineyard Land Bank has incorporated handicapped-accessible trails into their newer properties. Check the At-A-Glance Trip Planner on page vi.

Emergencies

Police, Fire, Ambulance: 911
Martha's Vineyard Hospital, Linton Lane, Oak Bluffs: 508-693-0410

At-a-Glance Trip Planner and Locator Map

The trip planner at the front of this guide preceding the Table of Contents allows you to find quickly the biking, walking, and paddling explorations that best suit your preferences. It lists routes that are appropriate for school-age children and also indicates where swimming and dogs are allowed. A quick check will reveal the length and level of difficulty of each exploration and whether there is an entry fee. Universal access areas are also noted.

The locator map pinpoints on the island the location of each off-road bike ride, walk, hike, or kayak trip. The numbers on the map correspond to the numbers of the trips.

Choosing Your Trip

Discover Martha's Vineyard contains forty-five trips. The first twenty acquaint you with places you can explore on foot, including towns, beaches, wildlife preserves, and conservation areas. The next thirteen trips describe rides for bicyclists—eight that tour the island on paved roads and five that go off-road to explore footpaths, bridle trails, and old carriage lanes. The fourth section of the book, Paddling, contains the best areas for kayaking and canoeing. Each trip directs you to a body of water and alerts you to special places to pull up your boat, swim, and explore.

Weather, location, age, and experience all help determine which trip you should choose. Before you start out on one of the explorations, read through the entire trip and look over the maps, which have been designed to use in conjunction with the written directions. The route is numbered to help guide you through each outing. Each successive number indicates a change in direction. If faced with choices and there are no number changes or directions, continue straight on the main path or road. Additional information—historical, botanical, and/or geological—comes after the direction. Skip to the next number to focus only on the directions. Most of the bike rides and walks loop in order to cover different terrain on your return.

The hiking, paddling, and off-road biking trips are grouped by town. All the sections include maps and specific directions and describe the geological, botanical, and historical features of each area.

Terminology

T intersection: The road on which you are traveling ends, requiring a right or left turn onto the intersected road. This junction forms a "T."
Bear or bend left or right: Turn at a wide angle (about 120°).
Merge: The road or trail joins another road.

Useful Gear

Before setting out on your exploration, make sure you have the necessary gear. The following is a checklist of useful items:

Insect repellent
Water
Sunscreen
Sunglasses
Tissues
Money
High-energy snacks
Bandanna or small hand towel
Small first-aid kit
Windbreaker
Towel, if swimming destination
Long pants, if wooded destination

Optional but useful equipment for cyclists:

Bike lock
Tool kit
Odometer
Handlebar bag with transparent map holder

Up-Island, Down-Island, Wet and Dry

Visitors are often confused by island terminology. If a place is referred to as "down-island," the location is the eastern end of the island in the towns of Edgartown, Vineyard Haven, or Oak Bluffs. Of those towns, Edgartown and Oak Bluffs are "wet," which means that their restaurants are permitted to serve liquor. If you go to dinner up-island, to Chilmark, West Tisbury, or Aquinnah, you may want to bring your own wine or beer because those towns are dry.

1
Walking and Hiking Martha's Vineyard

Choosing a Trip

Martha's Vineyard is blessed with a multitude of reservations, preserves, wildlife refuges, and sanctuaries. As a result, opportunities for walking and hiking abound. I have chosen my favorite properties based on scenery, location, and size, as well as for historical, botanical, and archaeological interest.

Since hiking allows for a more leisurely examination of the habitat than biking, these trips contain more botanical information. Here you will find words in **bold-face type** that point out a noteworthy site, tree, bush, flower, seashell, or fowl that often has accompanying drawings for help in identification.

Although each trip has been pretested, words and directions can be misinterpreted and intersection markers may be missing. If you lose your way, don't worry; rediscovering the route is part of the adventure.

In order to preserve what nature has kindly bestowed, please stay on marked trails, leave nothing behind, and take out only what you bring in.

Conservation Agencies

A number of conservation agencies own land on Martha's Vineyard. The largest is the Martha's Vineyard Land Bank Commission, which is funded by a 2 percent fee on real estate transactions. Each year the Land Bank acquires more land. At the time of publication it oversees 67 properties, totaling 2,900 acres.

The mission of the Sheriff's Meadow Foundation is to conserve, administer, and manage natural habitats for wildlife and all other lands that represent the natural character of Martha's Vineyard. It has conserved 2,300 acres.

The Trustees of Reservations preserves, for public use and enjoyment, properties of exceptional scenic, historic, and ecological value. It owns and manages five properties on Martha's Vineyard, totaling more than 2,000 acres.

Other smaller conservation agencies that preserve land on the island are the Vineyard Conservation Society, the Vineyard Open Land Foundation, The Massachusetts Audubon Society, and The Nature Conservancy.

Poison Ivy

Even a spot as wonderful as the Vineyard presents potential problems. To avoid **poison ivy**, which grows all over the island, you have to know what it looks like—clusters of three green leaves that are shiny if the plant grows in a sunny spot and dull if it is in the shade. In autumn the leaves turn bright red and the plant sprouts white berries. The ivy can grow like a vine, circling a tree trunk, or it can spread along the ground among bushes or on sand dunes. If your skin comes into contact with poison ivy, wash the affected areas with strong soap as soon as possible.

Poison ivy　　　　　　*Deer tick*　　　　　　*Dog tick*

Ticks

Ticks live on tall beach grass and in brushy areas. You often can see them hanging onto the tips of grass or leaves waiting to grab onto a warm-blooded traveler. These arachnids come in two varieties, the pinhead-size deer tick and the 1/4-inch dog tick. They usually attach to legs and then move upward. It takes them from 4 to 48 hours to break through the skin. If left undetected, the tick can swell to an inch in size and is capable of transmitting a number of diseases. Lyme disease, carried by the deer tick, is the one that people fear the most.

To prevent a tick from attaching to your skin, wear long pants tucked into high socks when walking or pedaling through tall grass or bushy areas. Avoid hiking through any untracked patches of brush. Walk in the middle of trails and avoid brushing against foliage. Use high strength DEET repellent on your clothing. Wear light-colored clothing, so you can see if any ticks are on you. They are easy to remove if they haven't attached. Always examine yourself thoroughly when you return home, especially the scalp, legs, and underarms.

If you find a tick on you, do not panic! Most ticks do not carry disease. Pull off the tick by grasping its head and pulling upward. Dispose of the tick by immersing it in alcohol or soapy water, and then wash your hands thoroughly. If you develop a skin rash around the bite and /or flu-like symptoms, see a doctor and tell him or her about the tick bite. Antibiotics are effective in the early treatment of Lyme disease.

TRIP 1
EDGARTOWN AND LIGHTHOUSE BEACH

Location: Edgartown

Rating: Easy: level walking on sidewalks and sand.

Distance: 3.4 miles to explore the town and beach, 1.7 miles to tour only the town.

Restrooms: On the left side of the Visitors' Center on Church Street, between Main Street and Pease's Point Way.

Food And Drink: Lattanzi Café, next to the Visitor's Center on Church Street, Among the Flowers Café on Mayhew Lane, off North Water Street (reasonable outdoor dining), Mad Martha's, North Water Street (ice cream, grinders).

Fees: Vincent House (hourly guided tours), Vineyard Museum, Old Whaling Church and Daniel Fisher House.

Tour the town center and then head for Lighthouse Beach to appreciate Edgartown's rare combination of charm, history, and beauty.

Directions

If you are arriving by car, forget hunting for a parking place (with a two-hour time limit), and park in the free Triangle Lot, located off the Edgartown-Vineyard Haven Road, just west of the triangle intersection with Beach Road. The small, free #11 Vineyard Transit Authority bus runs every 15 minutes from the parking lot to Edgartown Center. If you prefer to walk, the Triangle Lot is 0.5 mile from the starting point.

Trip Description

To fully appreciate Edgartown's assets, stroll down its narrow streets, lined with majestic old, meticulously landscaped homes. While walking along the beach to Eel Pond, you may notice other aspects of the town—elegant captains' homes perched above the shore, boats sailing in and out of Edgartown Harbor, and the rustic coast of Chappaquiddick and Cape Poge. Wear your bathing suit. Swimming, shelling, sunbathing and picnicking are at hand on this unspoiled stretch of sand.

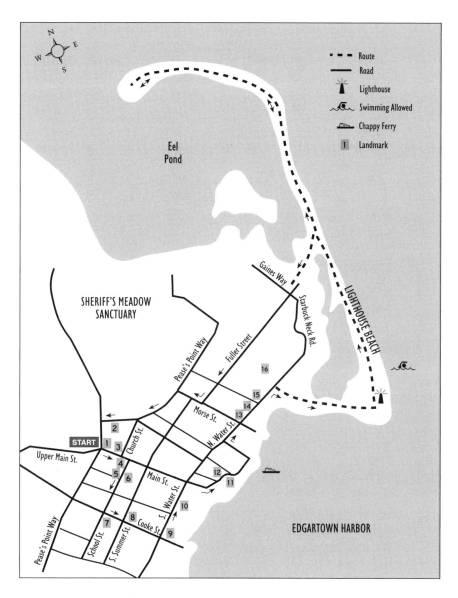

The Route

1. Begin at the intersection of Pease's Point Way and Main Street, and head east on Main Street.

Look on your left for the **Daniel Fisher House** (number 1 on the map). The simple yet elegant style of this home, with its symmetry and delicately carved mantels and moldings, is characteristic of the fine craftsmanship exhibited during the Federal period. Harvard-educated, Daniel Fisher arrived on the island in 1824 intending to practice medicine, but he eventually became the Vineyard's most successful businessman. He was a whale oil merchant who owned and operated the largest spermaceti (whale oil extract) candle factory in the world. As founder and first president of the Martha's Vineyard National Bank, Dr. Fisher became part owner of many whaling vessels. He also ran a whale oil refinery, a hardtack bakery that supplied whalers, a gristmill in West Tisbury, and even managed to squeeze in a small medical practice. He was described in 1857 as "the tallest, strongest-built, healthiest and handsomest, as well as the wealthiest and most influential inhabitant of Martha's Vineyard." The house built for him is now owned by the Martha's Vineyard Preservation Trust, Inc. and is a popular spot for weddings.

2. Walk behind the Daniel Fisher House to visit the simple, functional gray-shingled **Vincent House** (2), one of the oldest unaltered homes on the Vineyard.

Built in 1672 by William Vincent as a farmhouse near the shore of Edgartown Great Pond, it housed generations of Vincents until it was sold in 1941. The house was moved in 1977 and then carefully restored. The restorers deliberately left part of the interior unfinished so visitors could view the method of construction used in these early homes. Each of three rooms is furnished to represent a century of island life. Run by the Martha's Vineyard Preservation Trust, the Vincent House is open Monday through Friday from 11 A.M. to 3 P.M., May 1 through October 15.

3. From the Vincent house, cut through the parking lot in back of the **Old Whaling Church** (3) and turn right on Church Street. The Old Whaling Church is a fine example of Greek Revival architecture, with distinctive imposing columns interspersed with four large Gothic windows. This handsome structure, one of three churches designed by Frederick Baylies, Jr. of Edgartown, was constructed in the same manner as a whaling ship. Fifty-foot red pine beams support the church, which was the largest on the island when built in 1843. The light in its 92-foot tower could be seen far across the sea and served as a beacon for returning sailors. However, its large Methodist congregation gradually dwindled and the church became the property of the Martha's Vineyard Preservation Trust. Elegant old whale-oil lamps, now electrified, illuminate the 800-seat building, which today functions as both a church and a performing arts center.

4. From Main Street take your first right onto School Street. To the right, at number 20, sits the second church designed by Baylies in 1839 (4). When it functioned as a **Baptist Church**, it had a boxlike steeple. It was converted into the Masonic temple in 1925 and then to a private residence in 1979.

Next door at number 26 stands the **Jared Coffin House** (5), decorated with an ornate cornice and elegant portico. It was built in 1823 by Jared Coffin, one of Edgartown's master craftsmen.

Across the street at number 25 is the **Holmes Coffin House** (6), also built by Jared for his brother, Holmes, a mason, who formed the foundation for both houses.

5. Walk two blocks and turn left on Cooke Street. At the corner of School and Cooke Streets stand four buildings owned and operated by the Martha's Vineyard Historical Society. **The Vineyard Museum** (7), which includes the Thomas Cooke House and Foster Maritime Gallery, is open during summer, Monday through Saturday from 11 A.M. to 5 P.M. Guided tours are offered at 11 A.M. and 2 P.M. There is an entrance fee.

Thomas Cooke, a businessman and the Edgartown customs collector, built the Cooke House in 1766 to hold his office and family. At that time there were no houses between it and the ocean. Much of the eleven-room residence, including many of the windowpanes, has remained unchanged. Inside, exhibits feature collections of historic relics, including Native American artifacts, costumes, household goods, and marble headstones from the graves of two favorite chickens that belonged to Nancy Luce, an eccentric former resident of West Tisbury.

The Gale Huntington Library of History and the Foster Gallery are located in the main building. Inside the library hangs a portrait of wealthy Dr. Fisher. More than 10,000 books on Vineyard history and more than 100 logbooks from whaling vessels line the walls. The gallery displays items from the island's marine history, such as scrimshaw from whaling trips, ship models, and paintings.

A third building houses a hand-pumped 1852 fire engine, a peddler's cart, a racing boat and a Noman's Land boat, while the Francis Pease House contains the children's museum, museum shop, and restrooms. The brick tower in the middle of the lawn holds the gigantic Fresnel lens, which in 1854 was installed in the old Gay Head Lighthouse.

6. Go east on Cooke Street toward the waterfront. On the left side, where Summer Street intersects Cooke Street, stands the first church designed by Frederick Baylies. Founded by Governor Thomas Mayhew and his son, the **Federated Church** (8) was built in 1828. Baptist-Congregational services are held each Sunday in its spartan sanctuary, the oldest on the island. Look in the windows to see hanging whale-oil lamps, an old organ, and enclosed pews that were designed to trap heat during cold winter months.

7. Continue on Cooke Street for another block until you reach South Water Street. Turn left. On the right side at number 55 (9) stands a much enlarged version of one of the most historic houses in Edgartown. **John Coffin** left Nantucket in 1682 and built this home facing the harbor. Although it had only one story and measured 24 by 32 feet, Coffin worked out of his home as a blacksmith.

Walk another block to the **Captain Thomas Milton House**, on the right. Now owned by the Harborside Inn, the residence was built by Captain Thomas Milton, a retired sea captain who made most of his money investing in Edgartown real estate. In 1840 he built this house next to the flame tree that he had purchased as a seedling on one of his whaling trips to China. This huge, handsome tree is known as "**The Pagoda Tree**" (10) and is said to be the oldest one of its kind on this continent.

Proceed up South Water Street to the heart of the business district.

Whaling and Edgartown

Edgartown owes its prosperous beginnings to the whaling industry. Many of the English settlers who came to Martha's Vineyard in 1642 were familiar with whaling; others learned from the Wampanoag Tribe, who had been whaling for centuries. The Wampanoag killed whales for their meat, while the English were mainly after blubber, containing a valuable oil that was used for illumination and lubrication. In 1846 the United States whaling fleet boasted 735 ships out of 900 in the world and Edgartown was one of the primary nineteenth-century whaling ports. Like petroleum today, whaling made many people very wealthy. Edgartown's handsome homes were constructed during this period by residents who prospered because of the whaling industry. However, by 1860 petroleum and its derivatives had begun to replace whale oil, the main product delivered by whaling ships to ports up and down the coast. This reduced demand for whale oil, and coupled with a diminishing whale population, forced Edgartown residents to turn from whaling to the less remunerative occupations—fishing and navigating.

Follow the path to the Edgartown Lighthouse and Lighthouse Beach.

8. Take the first right back onto Main Street to proceed to the waterfront.

9. Turn left to reach **Memorial Wharf** (11), the town dock once owned by Dr. Fisher.

Located on the water beyond a cluster of stores, the wharf features an observation deck where you can climb up to view a magnificent seascape encompassing Cape Poge to the left, Chappaquiddick ahead, Katama Bay to the right, and Edgartown Harbor in the foreground.

Across the street from the wharf sits a small park dedicated to whales! Among the items displayed is a life-size sculpture of a whale's tail by Ovid Osborton Ward, in honor of his great-grandfather, who owned whaling ships. Next to the park sits the **Old Sculpin Gallery** (12). This quaint building originally belonged to entrepreneurial Dr. Fisher and was part of his whale oil refinery. After the demise of the whale oil industry, the building became a boat shop. This edifice has changed little during the last 200 years; if you step inside you can see the old floor and weathered beams, along with pictures painted by Vineyard artists.

Just past Memorial Wharf, on the right, two ferries motor to Chappaquiddick. During the busy summer months, each ferry—transporting bicycles, foot passengers, and three cars—continually shuttles back and forth across the narrow channel. Since one or the other ferry is always at or near one of the two docks, they are aptly named, "On Time."

10. From the ferry dock, turn left and travel up Daggett Street, past the line of cars patiently waiting for their turn to travel across the water to Chappaquiddick.

11. Turn right onto North Water Street to view the stately old Federal-style homes, positioned at an angle to the street so their occupants would have a better view of boats sailing into the harbor. On the roofs are "widows walks," or parapets, surrounded by balustrade railings, from which watchful spouses awaited the return of their seafaring husbands.

Many of these homes were built between 1830 and 1850 when the whaling industry was at its peak. Their uniformity of color, proper sense of proportion, and elegant architectural details combine to create one of the most aesthetically pleasing avenues on the Vineyard.

Number 86, which belonged to **Captain Jared Fisher** (13), is one of the most elegant homes. Its Greek Revival style indicates that it was built at the same time as the Daniel Fisher House. The Society for the Preservation of New England Antiquities now oversees the house.

Next door on the left is yet another Coffin House, this one having belonged to **Captain Edwin Coffin** (14). Built in 1840, it is identical to number 86 except it is missing the top floor.

When these houses were built, Edgartown was mostly open land. No homes stood on the water side of the street, and farmland occupied the area west of Water Street.

Strict regulations in this historic district stipulate that all homes must be covered by either white clapboard or gray shingles; doors and shutters must be black or dark green. Peek into the side and backyards of these homes to see carefully cultivated gardens where a variety of colorful blooms thrive in the moist salt air.

The **Captain Joseph Swazey House** (15), built in 1766, is considered one of the oldest houses in the area. Now boasting both an upper deck and lower porch, it originally had only one long porch where the occupants would gather on a summer evening to watch other residents stroll by. Swazey, the son of the Portuguese ambassador to England, sailed here from Lisbon determined to make his living on Martha's Vineyard.

The imposing building situated on the corner of North Water Street and Starbuck Neck Road is the **Harbor View Hotel** (16). Built in the 1890s, it was the first large hotel built on the island and was instrumental in converting Ed-

| Mussel | Scallop | Quahog |

gartown to a resort community. Across the street from the hotel are bike racks and white stone benches in front of a path leading to the lighthouse.

12. Turn right onto the path to the **Edgartown Lighthouse**, located at the entrance to Edgartown Harbor.

Originally, the lighthouse was built in 1828 on an island artificially constructed of granite blocks, connected by a wooden walkway to the mainland. The walkway was replaced by a causeway that became unnecessary when strong water currents created a small barrier beach and sandy access strip.

The seascape to your right reveals windsurfers' brightly colored sails weaving around anchored yachts, sailboats racing across the bay, and the "On Time" ferries shuttling back and forth to Chappaquiddick. The view toward Chappaquiddick includes bathers at the Chappy Beach Club, people fishing, and wood-shingled homes straddling the bluffs.

The multifaceted landscape up toward the large captains' homes includes yachts attached to docks and small boathouses hugging the water.

13. Head left down the mile-long stretch toward Eel Pond, where you'll have a closer view of narrow Cape Poge.

This isolated peninsula is accessible only by boat or by driving 7 miles on a sandy beach. The abundance of fish in Cape Poge Bay draws not only people fishing, but also flocks of seagulls that breed on the uninhabited western tip. If you make the trip to Cape Poge in June, beware of dive-bombing mother gulls protecting their young.

Eel Pond is great for kayaking (Trip 35) and a favorite island spot for shellfishing. Among the varieties of shells found on the beach are hard, round **quahog** shells, small, fragile **steamer** shells, black oval **mussel** shells, and ridged, fan-shaped **scallop** shells. Low tide draws clammers raking and plunging for these succulent mollusks. Each town has its own shellfish warden who issues permits for both clamming and scalloping, and who also polices the local waters.

The beach bends toward Eel Pond. At the tip of the beach you can view Oak Bluffs to the north. The Cape Poge Lighthouse sits off to the East on an elbow of land.

14. At the point where the narrow beach widens, look for a path that leads to Gaines Way. Turn left on this path.

15. Turn left onto Gaines Way.

16. Bear right onto Fuller Street. Flower lovers should watch for colorful gardens hiding behind fences.

17. Fuller ends at Morse Street. Turn right.

18. At the next block Morse intersects with Pease's Point Way. Turn left.

19. Follow Pease's Point Way, past the bike racks and trolley stop, as it bends left and then intersects with Upper Main Street.

20. Turn right on Upper Main Street to return to the starting point.

TRIP 2
SHERIFF'S MEADOW SANCTUARY

Location: Edgartown
Rating: Easy
Distance: 0.5 mile
Food and Drink: On Upper Main Street near Cannonball Park: Soigné for gourmet take-out. Edgartown Center offers many choices.
Restrooms: Located on the left side of the Visitors' Center on Church Street, which lies between Main Street and Pease's Point Way.

Although Sheriff's Meadow is located in the heart of Edgartown, this small scenic sanctuary hosts a range of natural communities usually found miles from civilization.

Directions
To reach the sanctuary from the Main Street side of Cannonball (Memorial) Park in Edgartown, go north on Pease's Point Way. Continue straight on Pease's Point Way, which then becomes Planting Field Way. Proceed 0.2 mile down Planting Field Way. Look for the small Sheriff's Meadow sign on the right side of the road.

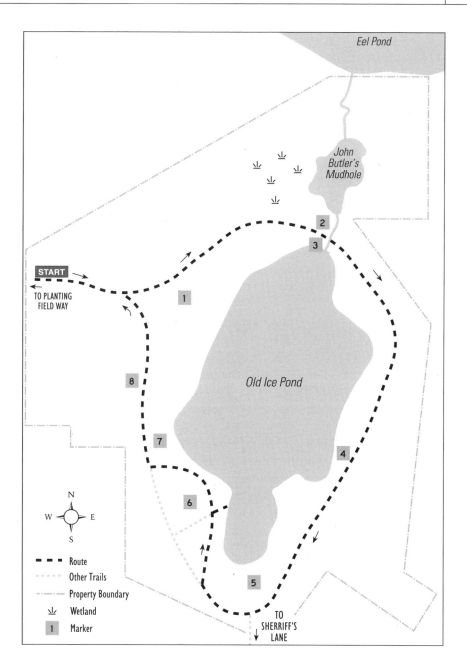

Trip Description

Here you'll find meadow and woodland, freshwater pond and saltwater marsh—diverse environments supporting a wide variety of flora and fauna.

The sanctuary's trails wind through lush foliage, revealing views across Eel Pond to Nantucket Sound and Chappaquiddick. Perhaps because Sheriff's Meadow is so close to the hustle and bustle of Edgartown, the variety and number of bird calls are all the more noticeable. Bring your binoculars on your walk so that you can spot birds such as black-bellied plovers, red-winged blackbirds, or great blue herons. You may also glimpse a raccoon crawling through the brush or spy several swans flying from one body of water to the next.

The Route

1. Proceed down the pine-needle-covered path shaded by **eastern white pine** and **spruce** trees.

2. The trail forks just as you enter a meadow. Go left.

You will pass several large **white oak** trees with smooth pale gray trunks. Baby **Norway spruce** trees grow under the canopy of pine and **northern white cedar** trees.

Watch for poison ivy along the path as it bends, crossing between John Butler's Mud Hole on the left and Sheriff's Pond on the right. A bench beside the path invites you to sit and admire the view beyond the cattails. Tall plants with hot dog-like tops, **cattails** provide both food and shelter for wildlife. Humans also can feast on the plant by boiling the top, which is filled with unripe pollen spikes, and eat it like corn on the cob. Its greens and roots are also edible.

The #3 marker on the right refers to Sheriff's Pond. Both the sanctuary and pond were named for a former owner of this property, Isaiah Pease, who was sheriff of Dukes County from 1822 until his death in 1862. The sheriff sold ice from this freshwater pond for refrigeration and built an icehouse nearby where he cut and packed the ice in straw to keep it frozen during summer.

Beyond the Mud Hole lies Eel Pond, one of the kayaking destinations (Trip 35), which is encircled by Little Beach. If you look far out onto Nan-

Northern white cedar

Sea lavender

Tamarack

tucket Sound you'll spot the Cape Poge Lighthouse on an elbow of land connected to Chappaquiddick by a stretch of barrier beach.

Peeking out from the marsh grass is **sea lavender**. Its name refers to the color of its tiny flowers that bloom in late summer and early fall. Also flowering in autumn is **seaside goldenrod.** Its small bright yellow flowers form a rod-like cluster at the top. The **groundsel tree** also favors these marshy areas. In late summer and early fall it produces clusters of small, white, feathery flowers.

As you proceed around the west side of the pond, you'll notice that the vegetation becomes very dense. Non-native plant species, with their jungle-like density of vines, stems, and runners, are crowding out native species. The Sheriff's Meadow Foundation is attempting to reduce this invasion of Asiatic bittersweet, Japanese honeysuckle, and porcelain berry.

Remain on the main trail while passing side paths to private homes and to the tennis courts at the Edgartown Yacht Club. Opposite the path to the tennis courts on the right side of the path grows a **tamarack** tree, a conifer that sheds its leaves in winter. This tree is easy to spot because its slender needles grow in large tufts that shoot out at the ends of stunted branches. Native Americans used the tough fibers from its roots to bind the seams of their birch bark canoes. The wood of the tamarack tree is now used for poles and lumber. You will not find many other tamarack trees on the island, as this species generally prefers a colder climate.

On the right, by the #4 marker, a cleared area encourages a stop at the edge of the pond to view the wildlife. See if you can spot painted turtles sunning themselves on logs or snapping turtles gliding through the water.

Henry Beetle Hough

Much of the land in the 17-acre Sheriff's Meadow Sanctuary originally belonged to Henry Beetle Hough, a respected island resident who for many years was editor and publisher of the weekly newspaper, the *Vineyard Gazette*. In order to protect this property from future development, Henry and his wife, Betty, created the Sheriff's Meadow Foundation in 1958 and donated 11 acres of the land that surrounds Sheriff's Pond. During the next fifteen years, other landowners donated six additional acres to the sanctuary. Today, the Sheriff's Meadow Foundation has grown into a conservation organization with island holdings of more than 2,000 acres.

From the trail you can see a view of John Butler's Mudhole, Eel Pond, and Lighthouse Beach.

Kingfishers, cormorants, and terns often swoop down to snatch small minnows while swans, mallards, and Canada geese paddle around in their never-ending search for food.

3. Pass the left fork that leads to private residences and follow the trail through a pine forest.

4. At the next fork, turn right toward the pond. A bench, perched near the water's edge, provides a resting place where you can appreciate this tranquil setting.

A boardwalk lies between the #7 marker on the right and #8 on the left. Number 7 refers to **water willow**, a tall plant that produces small fuchsia flowers in July. Number 8 marks a **shrub swamp** where water level rises during very wet weather. Species that grow here, such as highbush blueberry, swamp azalea, sweet pepperbush, and poison sumac, thrive in the acidic soils of these swamps.

5. Return to the main trail to continue the loop.

Sensitive fern, which also prefers a moist environment, grows beside the trail.

6. Bear left to return to the entrance to the sanctuary.

TRIP 3
CAROLINE TUTHILL WILDLIFE PRESERVE

Location: Edgartown
Rating: Easy: mostly level walking with a few short inclines.
Distance: 1.4 miles
Food and Drink: The Triangle shopping area has many options.

The Caroline Tuthill Wildlife Preserve is just a stone's throw from the hustle and bustle of the Triangle shopping area, but its hiking trails through 154 acres of pine forest and meadow give it the feeling of being far removed from civilization.

Directions
From the Triangle intersection at Beach Road, travel west 0.4 mile on the Edgartown-Vineyard Haven Road, or travel 3.7 miles east from the blinker intersection at Barnes Road. The preserve and its small parking area are located on the north side of the road.

Trip Description
This preserve, one of Martha's Vineyard's hidden treasures, was donated by John and Nora Tuthill in memory of their daughter, Caroline, and is administered by the Sheriff's Meadow Foundation. Even long-time residents are not aware of its hiking trails along the shore of scenic Sengekontacket Pond and the opportunities for bird-watching around the salt marsh. If you are looking for a conveniently located spot with varied but not taxing terrain that offers fields of lady's slippers in spring and succulent blueberries and huckleberries in summer, head for the Caroline Tuthill Preserve.

The Route

1. Start on the path behind the signpost.
   Soon after you begin your hike you'll see a small #1 wooden sign posted in front of evergreen sprouts on the left side of the trail. These sprouts reveal why **pitch pine** trees grow all over the island. Underneath the sprouts are

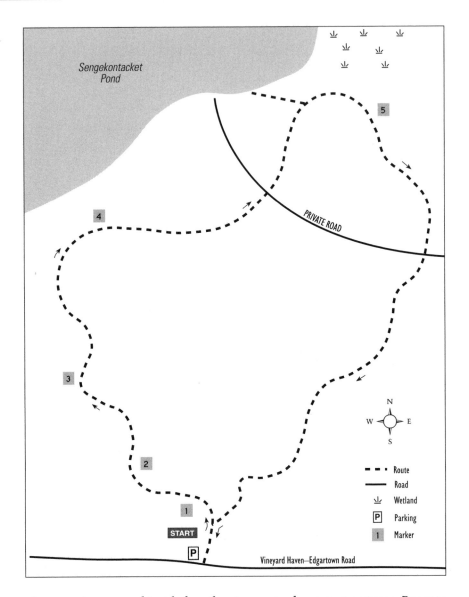

pine tree stumps, and just below the stumps are large root systems. Because these large vigorous roots grow close to the surface, they can quickly issue new sprouts in an open area where fire or wind has destroyed older pines.

2. Bear left on the trail that winds through a grove of oaks and then pines.

As you walk up an incline, watch on both the left and right of the trail for crunchy gray-blue moss-like clumps growing in open sunny spots. These primitive plants, which have no roots, stems, leaves or flowers, are a species of **lichens** called ***Cladonia***. They are often found in areas with severe climatic conditions.

Lichens, which have been around for millions of years, are comprised of two separate organisms: fungus and alga. Both organisms work together like a well-coached team, performing different functions that allow survival in hot arid regions as well as frigid wind-blown mountaintops. The fungus protects and supplies moisture to the plant while the alga provides food.

Cladonia feel sharp and brittle if they grow in hot, dry conditions or soft and spongy if they have absorbed water. If you have any extra water with you, put a very small piece of the dry lichen in a cup with a little water. Watch it quickly absorb all the liquid. This nifty moisture conservation trick demonstrates how lichens can survive during years of drought and extreme heat or cold. *Cladonia* may not mind extreme weather conditions but it is very fussy about air quality; it refuses to grow in polluted areas. Naturally, Vineyarders are particularly partial to this plant because it reinforces their belief that their relatively unpolluted island provides better living conditions than the mainland.

Ignore the path emerging on the left and continue walking straight, following both the yellow-topped wooden trail markers and the yellow blazes nailed to trees.

Lady's Slippers

If you are walking in late May or early June, glance under the pine trees for lady's slippers, orchids that grow only in the acidic soil supplied by pine needles. Thousands bloom in this preserve, but their delicate pink blossoms are scarce elsewhere. They are practically impossible to propagate and almost equally difficult to pollinate. A lady's slipper does not reward a pollinator with nectar. It must rely on a not-so-smart bumblebee to enter through a small slit in its slipper-like pouch and then proceed deep within the flower to find the anther. When the nectarless bee exits through a hole in the rear wall of the flower, it rubs against the anther, which then releases the pollen. If the bee is to deposit the pollen, it must go on the same unrewarding search in another lady's slipper. In summer you will see only pollinated plants because they keep their shriveled seed pods. Plants not pollinated dry up and die.

Lady's slipper

The trail approaches Sengekontacket Pond and then bends to the right, following the shore. Here you'll have a view of the pond, the beach, Nantucket Sound and Beach Road. To the north you can see the town of Oak Bluffs perched on the headland that juts out into the water.

As the trail gets closer to the water and the land becomes moister, the vegetation changes. The fragrant **sweet pepperbush** exhibits spiky clusters of small white flowers that perfume the summer air.

3. Cross a dirt road and continue on the trail until you reach a T intersection. Turn left onto a narrow side path if you wish to visit a small sandy beach that offers a panorama of Sengekontacket Pond and Nantucket Sound.

4. Retrace your steps on the side path and proceed straight at the intersection. Ahead on the right behind the #5 marker lies a salt marsh. On the opposite side of the trail sits a bench conveniently located for observing the wildlife. Plants and algae growing in the marsh provide nutrients for both shellfish and finfish, which in turn draw shorebirds. You may spot **snowy egrets**, white birds with long black legs and long black bills, or **great blue herons**, with long curved necks and dagger-like bills.

Mallards also frequent salt marshes. Instead of diving into the water to feed, they tip their heads down, forcing their tails to bob up in the air. The male is easy to spot because he sports a white necklace below his dark green neck and head.

The view from the salt marsh lookout includes two small bodies of water, both named Trapp's Pond. Beyond the ponds, lying far out in Nantucket Sound, is Cape Poge Elbow. This skinny strip of land, extending out from Chappaquiddick, is a prime fishing spot and a seagull spawning area. Both Trapp's Pond and Cape Poge Bay can be explored by kayak. (See Trips 38 and 39).

After you leave the marsh view, look on the right for four dead oak trees. In the same area you'll see a group of baby pitch pines that have taken advantage of the newly available sunlight.

Pitch pine

Mallard

Sweet pepperbush

Perfect place for a shady stroll on a hot day.

5. Cross back over the road and remain on the trail as it passes huckleberry, blueberry, and bayberry bushes. During summer, the **huckleberry**'s small pale flower becomes a dark round berry containing a tiny seed that crunches when chewed. The **blueberry** has a frosty covering and does not crunch. The **bayberry** bush has larger oval leaves and only the female develops clusters of small, round, hard, white berries that are attached directly to the stem. Huckleberries and blueberries provide a tasty snack for the hungry hiker. Bayberries, which are tiny and rock hard, remain on the bush all winter and help sustain the island bird population during cold weather.

Just before the trail starts to descend, look for a small kettle hole on the left side surrounded by a thicket of highbush blueberries. **Kettle holes** were formed by glacial action. About 15,000 years ago, when the glacier that covered the northeastern section of the United States started to recede, immense blocks of ice broke off. These blocks then became buried in all the debris that the glacier had picked up on its southward journey. Because these huge chunks melted more slowly than the rest of the ice, they left large depressions in the earth. Some of these kettle holes were so deep that they filled with water and became small inland ponds.

6. After climbing up and down a small hill, bear left at the fork to return to the entrance.

TRIP 4
FELIX NECK WILDLIFE SANCTUARY

Location: Edgartown
Rating: Easy: wide flat trails
Distance: 1.5 miles
Restrooms: In the Nature Center where you pay your admission fee.
Fees: $4.00 adult; $3.00 children; free to members of the
Massachusetts Audubon Society. Free guided tours Monday
through Friday from 2:30 P.M.to 3:30 P.M.

**Take a walk on the wild side! All manner of wildlife nest,
breed, and forage in and around this 350-acre sanctuary.**

Directions
From the triangle intersection in Edgartown, travel 2 miles west on the Edgartown-Vineyard Haven Road. From the junction with State Road in Vineyard Haven, the distance is 4.2 miles east on the same road. A Massachusetts Audubon sign marks the entrance on the north side of the road. Drive 0.7 mile down the dirt road or bike/walk on the dirt path to the parking lot.

Trip Description
As you explore the sanctuary, mallards, Canada geese, osprey, or a horseshoe crab may accompany you on wide level trails along beach and salt marsh, through open fields and woodlands. Birders describe this Massachusetts Audubon Society property as one of the prime island locales for observing more than 100 species of native birds. Felix Neck also provides an assortment of naturalist-led activities, from bird and wildlife identification walks to seashore explorations and kayak trips. Apply plenty of mosquito repellent.

The Route
An osprey pole stands next to the entrance road. **Osprey,** which resemble eagles, prefer to nest on top of dead trees near water that supports a plentiful supply of fish. Until recently, a lack of suitable trees prevented osprey from building nests on the island. Gus Ben David, the former director of

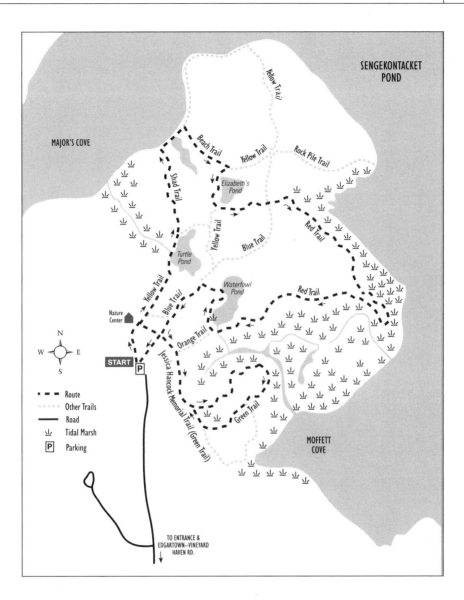

Felix Neck, was instrumental in increasing the number of osprey by encouraging the telephone company and local volunteers to erect telephone poles for nesting sites. There are now more than 60 pairs of osprey located all over the island.

1. On your way from the parking lot to the Nature Center, stop at the butterfly garden, where butterflies sip nectar from flowers planted specifically

Horshoe crab shell and scallop shell found on driftwood on the beach at Felix Neck.

to attract them. A goldfish pond lies next to the garden. Brightly hued fish swim among water hyacinths and lilies.

The Nature Center contains trail maps, an exhibit room, and a shop selling books and nature-oriented items. The exhibit room features displays as well as fresh and saltwater aquariums filled with native fish, bivalves, amphibians, and reptiles. A video camera focuses on a barn owl so viewers can see first hand what an owl does during the day.

Begin your hike on the Yellow Trail, also named the Sassafras Trail, which starts behind the Nature Center.

The field on your right is mowed to provide an environment for wildflowers, butterflies, birds, and small mammals. If you are hiking during the summer months, look for the brilliant orange flower called **butterfly weed**. Its name is derived from its frequent companion, the monarch butterfly, which dines on its clusters of five curved and five upright petals. This plant also is called **pleurisy root** because Native Americans chewed its roots to alleviate the lung condition we now know as pleurisy.

2. Bear left, remaining on the Yellow Trail, to walk on a wooden boardwalk that crosses an artificial pond.

Although this body of water is named Turtle Pond because of the several painted turtles that live here, you are more apt to spot **Canada geese** than turtles. These large, web-footed birds are easy to identify because they have black heads and necks interrupted by thick white bands underneath their chins. Canada geese are monogamous and do not allow any deviation from their strict code. If a couple leaves the flock and the male returns without his mate, the other geese will chase him away.

3. Fork left onto the Shad Trail, so named because of the **shadbushes** growing under large oak and sassafras trees at the start of the trail.

Shadbush got its name from a coincidence of timing: In May, shadfish migrate upstream to spawn, and at the same time the shadbush's fragrant white flowers begin to bloom. Shadbush is also called Juneberry because its flower clusters turn into reddish-purple berries in June. This trail could also be named the Blueberry Trail because of the number of bushes that line the path.

4. The Shadbush Trail leads to an inlet of Sengekontacket Pond called Major's Cove.

Upon reaching the shore, turn right and follow the coast through a marshy area.

This marshland is the main reason why large numbers of shore birds summer on Felix Neck. **Cordgrass** and **salt marsh hay** provide food and shelter for both finfish and shellfish. They, in turn, draw many varieties of shorebirds. As you walk along the beach you'll find numerous shells, some cracked and some with beak holes, that have been discarded by our feathered friends.

Interspersed among the cordgrass grows **common glasswort**, distinguished by its cactus-like branches. A favorite of ducks and geese, glasswort was also popular with early settlers who used its stems for making pickles and sprinkled its branch tips in salads to add a salty flavor.

The water in Sengekontacket Pond is seeded for scallops and clams. During low tide you'll often see clammers raking up quahogs or digging for steamers. As you stroll along the shore, watch for clam, mussel, whelk, and scallop shells. You may also find the molt of a **horseshoe crab**. The molt, which looks like a dead horseshoe crab, is actually its cast-off shell—the crab outgrew its covering in the same way that a ten-year-old child's jacket fits for only one season. If you are not squeamish, pick up this strange looking arthropod and look for the little slit that the crab used as an escape hatch. Horseshoe crabs, like ticks, are arachnids, prehistoric fauna that have been around for thousands of years.

If you venture into the water, you may see green crabs with flat oval shells and spider crabs with spiny circular bodies. Check the bottom for mud snails, the pond's sanitary engineers. They clean the water by eating decayed organic matter that has settled on the pond floor.

5. Follow the shore until you come to the next opening. Turn right onto the Beach Trail.

6. At the intersection with the Yellow/Sassafras Trail, turn right.

7. Pass on the left another artificial body of water named Elizabeth's Pond and turn left onto the Red/ Marsh Trail.

This path travels through a pitch pine forest with an undercover of bayberry and huckleberry bushes. You'll notice that the trees and bushes are smaller and more deformed here than in the other areas of Felix Neck. Because this land is higher and less protected, its vegetation is continually bombarded by wind and salt spray.

This route skirts Sengekontacket Pond. Follow the sign that reads, "Sengekontacket Pond View."

The path next to the water appears to be a favorite shell dumping ground. Birds discard shells after devouring the mollusks inside. You may find a whelk shell—decorated with beak holes—to take home as a souvenir.

Across the water lies Sarson's Island, a nesting ground for **double-crested cormorants**. These birds are easy to spot because their dark color and long necks easily distinguish them from the light-colored sea gull. You often will see them sunning themselves on a rock or piece of land. Cormorants, unlike most water fowl, don't produce the oil that enables water to run off their feathers, so they are forced to spend much of their time drying their wings. **American oystercatchers**, an endangered species that has been protected, now occupy the southern half of the island. Their bright red beaks and black and white bodies make them easy to spot.

8. At the next junction, proceed straight, continuing on the Red Trail through the marsh toward the water, following the Pond View sign.

Great blue herons, long-legged, grayish-blue wading birds with pointed bills and long necks, frequently visit this area. **Mallards** often swim in and around the wetland. The male highlights his green head with a white neck ring, while the plainer female is covered by mottled brown feathers brightened by a white tail.

9. Proceed through this marshy section and circle back to rejoin the trail.

10. At the next junction, bear left and remain on the Red Trail.

11. Remain on the Red Trail until you come to a right turn that leads to the Waterfowl Pond and the waterfowl observation building, a tranquil spot to observe the wildlife.

12. From the waterfowl observation building, turn right, and follow the shore of the pond. The stone bench provides a convenient stop to rest and watch ducks paddle by.

13. Follow the path to the Old Farm Road/Blue Trail. Turn left on the road and then left again to head back to the parking lot.

If, after leaving the waterfowl observation building, you are interested in further investigation of the salt marsh, remain on the dirt road until you come to the junction with the Jessica Hancock Memorial Trail (Green Trail). Turn left. This short loop runs next to the marsh.

To return to the parking lot from the Hancock Trail, turn left onto the Red Trail.

TRIP 5
MYTOI GARDEN-EAST BEACH

Location: Chappaquiddick

Rating: Easy

Distance: 0.5 mile around the garden, 0.4 mile through the woods to the salt marsh.

Restrooms: At the east end of the Mytoi Parking Lot and also next to the gatehouse at Dike Bridge

Food and Drink: Chappy General Store, located 2.2 miles from the Chappy Ferry and 0.3 mile from Dike Road, sells snacks, drinks, and sandwiches. The kiosk at the entrance to Mytoi sells drinks. A water fountain sits to the left of the kiosk.

Fees: The entrance fee to East Beach is $3.00. Children under 12 and members of The Trustees of Reservations may enter for free.

Explore this Japanese-style garden, enjoying its unusual plantings, brooks, benches, and bridges. Continue on to East Beach, where you may spot a variety of shorebirds, including osprey and oystercatchers.

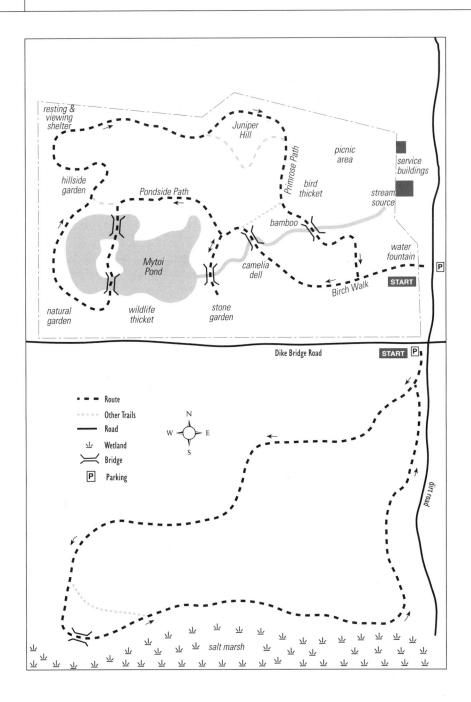

resting &
viewing
shelter

Juniper
Hill

picnic
area

service
buildings

hillside
garden

Pondside Path

Primrose Path

bird
thicket

stream
source

bamboo

water
fountain

Mytoi
Pond

camelia
dell

START

natural
garden

wildlife
thicket

stone
garden

Birch Walk

Dike Bridge Road

START

━ ━ Route

· · · · Other Trails

─── Road

⅄ Wetland

⌣ Bridge

P Parking

N
W   E
S

dirt road

salt marsh

Directions

From the Chappy Ferry, travel 2.5 miles on Chappaquiddick Road. When the road bends sharply to the right, continue straight onto unpaved Dike Road. Proceed 0.5 mile to Mytoi. The parking lot and bike rack are at the entrance to the reservation.

To reach Dike Bridge and East Beach from Mytoi, continue 0.2 mile farther down the road. A parking lot and bike rack are located just before the bridge.

Trip Description

Who would expect a Japanese-style garden to be tucked away on Chappaquiddick? Mytoi Garden grew from an unusual bequest: it stipulated the land be used to create a serene sanctuary, filled with unusual plantings, brooks, benches, and bridges. Across Dike Road a rustic trail serves as a contrast as it winds through woods that border a salt marsh.

East Beach, located at the end of Dike Road, offers isolation, beauty, and soft white sand.

The Route

1. Enter Mytoi under an arch built from tree trunks and limbs. The trail passes, on the left, **rhododendron bushes**, a cluster of **hay-scented ferns** and four varieties of birch trees: Himalayan, paper, European river, and heritage.

The garden contains native and exotic plants and trees that have been chosen to maintain visual interest throughout the year. **Witch hazel** blooms in February and March. During spring Mytoi is awash with color from the blooms of wild roses, rhododendrons, azaleas, daffodils, primrose, lady's slippers, and **dogwood** and stewartia trees. In summer, the purple petals of the Japanese iris decorate the pond. In autumn, look for white blossoms decorating the rare **franklinia tree**.

The opening on the right, displaying only a few large rocks, a simple waterfall, and ferns, sets the tranquil tone of the sanctuary. The designers wanted people who entered the sanctuary to leave behind the stresses of their lives and have a peaceful, relaxing experience.

A stone Japanese lantern on the left is a tribute to the founder of Mytoi, Hugh Jones. He began his project around 1958 and planted bushes, trees, and flowers and landscaped Mytoi in the style of Japanese gardens until he died in 1965. Mary Wakeman, a local conservationist, took over the project and continued to use Japanese design elements as she expanded on Jones' original

| *Rhododendron* | *Witch hazel* | *Dogwood* |

idea. In 1976 Mary Wakeman donated the Mytoi property to The Trustees of Reservations, a nonprofit conservation organization. Her gift included this 3 1/2-acre garden and 10 acres of pine forest across the road.

Passing through a wooden structure that serves to formally welcome you to the garden, proceed along a stone path, passing a bench on the left. The bench was one of the many donated by residents of Chappaquiddick. Next to the bench stands an unusual looking tree called with an even more unusual name: **threadleaf false cypress**.

2. After crossing a tiny stone bridge, turn left onto a path that ends at a rock garden adorned with a variety of groundcover. A bench facing Mytoi Pond encourages quiet contemplation.

3. Returning to the main path, turn left.

On the left side of the path sits a tiny **Japanese maple tree** with feathery russet-colored leaves. It provides a marked contrast in size, color, and leaf texture to its neighbor, a **blue atlas cedar tree**.

Highbush blueberry bushes overlook the pond. They ripen at the end of July and beginning of August. Feel free to pick the berries. In July, **Japanese iris** flaunt their purple blooms at the edge of the pond. In August, **pickerelweed** decorate the pond with their purple flowers.

4. Turn left to cross a footbridge that loops around the small island.

Wooden benches encourage you to sit, watch, and listen to the inhabitants of the pond. On the water you'll see whirligig beetles swimming in never-ending circles, while waterstriders are busily jumping from spot to spot. Look in the pond for goldfish and koi or painted and snapping turtles. Bright yellow markings on the head and neck of the painted turtle distinguish it from the snapping turtle. The croaking frogs blend so well with the background that you are more likely to hear than see them.

5. Return to the path and turn left. Proceed up the steps to the upper trail, passing a garden of groundcover, including cotoneaster, juniper, and bearberry.

The footbridge across Mytoi Pond.

6. A **weeping Alaskan cedar tree** stands on your left just before the Resting and Viewing Shelter constructed with black locust logs.

7. After ascending, look on your left at a **deodar cedar tree** next to a **dwarf hinoki cypress**. Across the path on the right is a **coral bark maple tree**.

8. After descending you will reach a bridge that crosses a narrow brook and tiny waterfall. They were created by digging channels to direct the flow of water from the well near the parking lot.

Across from the waterfall stands a **cryptomeria elegans tree** next to a **sweetbay magnolia**, which produces gorgeous white blossoms in early summer.

9. Bear right at the next junction to return to the entrance.

10. To walk through an environment that offers a marked contrast to this manicured garden, and to view wildlife around the saltmarsh, exit from the parking lot and cross Dike Road.

11. Head left down the dirt road and take the first right. The trail curves right and then bends left as it follows an inlet from Poucha Pond.

12. At the fork, bear right onto a side path for an unobstructed view of the birds and wildlife that inhabit the saltmarsh. You may spot otters scampering through the high grass named phragmites or **great blue herons**, **snowy egrets**, and black and white **American oystercatchers**, with bright orange bills, standing in the marsh.

13. Bear right to continue on the main trail.

14. Turn left onto the dirt road to return to the parking lot.

Dike Bridge—East Beach

Perhaps no other spot on Martha's Vineyard inspires as much curiosity as Dike Bridge, site of a tragedy involving Massachusetts Senator Edward Kennedy. In 1969, the senator drove his car off Dike Bridge. The vehicle sank into Poucha Pond, and the passenger, Mary Jo Kopechne, drowned; Kennedy survived. Tourists now flock to the spot, but most visitors are not aware that a world-class beach lies on the opposite side of the bridge. For more than a decade, Dike Bridge had not been passable and one could access East Beach only by paying a hefty fee to navigate a four-wheel-drive vehicle 2 miles from Wasque Reservation. The bridge reopened in 1995. Parking in the adjoining lot is limited to 24 cars.

If, after crossing Dike Bridge, you turn right and drive 2 miles, you will enter Wasque Reservation. If you turn left at East Beach, you will head in the direction of Cape Poge Wildlife Refuge. This isolated barrier beach travels north for 3 miles. On the right lies the Muskeget Channel in Nantucket Sound and on the left, Cape Poge Bay. A variety of shorebirds, including osprey, oystercatchers, least terns, and common terns, feed and nest in this area.

Among the vegetation that grows in this sandy soil is **sea rocket**, a member of the mustard family with large seed pods and fleshy leaves that taste like horseradish. **Eel grass**, which produces flowers only in salt water, grows near the marsh. The beach-loving *Rosa rugosa* decorates the dunes with its pink blossoms in spring and shiny red rose hips in summer and fall.

You may find people casting fishing lines on the outer shores of the refuge or boats carrying people fishing for scallops in the warm shallow water of Cape Poge Bay. Many varieties of gulls line the shore and plunge from the sky, competing for the abundant fish.

TRIP 6
WASQUE RESERVATION

Location: Chappaquiddick

Rating: Easy

Distance: 3 miles

Fees: Biking will eliminate the $3.00 car entrance fee; however, you will have to pay $3.00 per person to enter. Members of The Trustees of Reservations and children under 15 are admitted free. The round-trip fees to cross Edgartown Harbor on the ferry to Chappaquiddick are as follows: car and driver $12.00, bicyclist $6.00, walk-on or car passenger $3.00.

Restrooms: Located at the entrance, at the beach parking lot and at the parking lot near Wasque Point.

Food and Drink: Water pumps are located at both ends of the main parking lot. Wasque is a great place for picnicking, with lots of tables overlooking the water.

Here, you can hike to miles of secluded barrier beach that separate Wasque's southern tip from the Atlantic Ocean's dynamic surf, with waves to daunt the most intrepid body-surfer.

Directions
After debarking from the Chappy Ferry, follow the paved road for 4.5 miles. When the pavement turns to sand, continue for 0.7 mile. If you have a mountain or hybrid bike and can navigate this sandy section, you will avoid the possibility of facing a "filled to capacity" parking lot.

Trip Description
Calm Katama Bay, a haven for windsurfers and clammers, lies on the west side of Wasque (pronounced Way-skwee) Reservation. Poucha Pond and Muskeget Channel bound Wasque on the east. One of the properties owned by The Trustees of Reservations, Wasque offers mellow off-road biking, hiking, swimming, picnicking, and bird watching within its 200 acres.

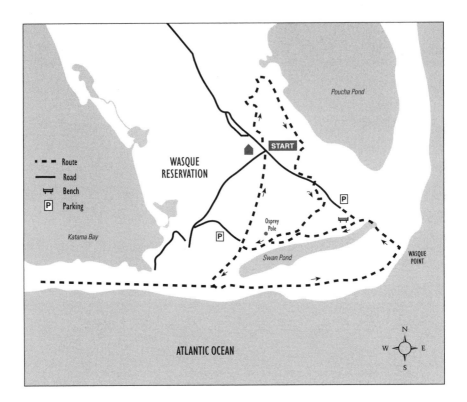

The Route

Wasque Reservation was formed about 15,000 years ago. Rivers of water flowed off a 10,000-foot glacier and deposited sand and gravel picked up as the glacier inched southward. This accumulation of sand and gravel formed the outwash plain that composes the south side of the island.

1. Begin at the trailhead east of the gatehouse and just behind a picnic bench.

Follow the wide pine-needle-covered trail (great for biking) as it runs through a pine forest and oak woodland. The trail enters a meadow and borders Poucha Pond. If you spot a large gray bird with a wide wing-span and a long curved neck, it's likely a great blue heron, a species that frequents the pond.

2. Upon reaching the dirt road turn left, following the Trail sign.

3. Proceed 0.2 mile and turn right onto a wood-chipped trail that cuts across sandplain grassland. The Trustees have cut the grassland to maintain this habitat.

| Great blue heron | Beachgrass | Dusty miller |

Stop for a minute in this scrubby heathland to appreciate the water views and investigate the flora. In spring, look for **trailing arbutus** which produces small clusters of pink or white flowers that give off a fragrant sweet smell. If you are visiting in late summer and fall, the heathland is dotted with **New York asters**, small lavender flowers with bright yellow centers.

4. The trail enters a forest of small pitch pine trees. After emerging, turn right at the T intersection, heading toward Swan Pond.

5. Bear right at the fork.

On the right, a high pole houses eagle-like **osprey** which often sit on their perch and scan the water for fish.

6. Continue straight as the path merges and widens, running parallel to Swan Pond.

As befits its name, Swan Pond often boasts a couple of graceful white **swans**. It's rare to see just one swan as they usually travel in pairs. In late spring and summer, you may see a couple with their cygnets paddling behind in a straight line. If the cygnets are under a year old, they will be covered with grayish-brown down. The females lay their eggs in large nests built with water plants that are lined with the down from the swans' bodies. Swans feed on seeds and roots of water plants, as well as shellfish and worms.

Swan Pond previously connected Poucha Pond on the east with Katama Bay on the west. However, each year the pond diminishes in size.

7. Bear left on the path heading toward the boardwalk. A bench provides a rest stop, if necessary, before you walk down the boardwalk to the beach.

This long wooden ramp guarantees that visitors will not stray into the fragile dune area. In order to stabilize the dunes, environmentalists encourage the growth of **beach grass**. Its strong root system helps to anchor the dune and prevent erosion. Notice that beach grass, which can withstand a harsh, windy, and salty environment, is the only vegetation growing on the steep seaward side of the dunes. The softer, more sloping inland or protected side of the dune hosts a variety of plants. Look for the delicate blue-gray **dusty miller** which produces small yellow flowers in summer. Its fuzzy, dusty-looking protective covering helps the plant conserve water so that it can grow in arid conditions. **Seaside goldenrod** is another plant that has adapted to this harsh environment. In fall it decorates the sand with clusters of bright yellow flowers.

8. Upon reaching the beach, you have a choice: you can turn right onto the barrier beach separating the ocean and Katama Bay or turn left toward Wasque Point.

If you walk west toward Katama Bay, be aware of the tern nesting areas. **Least terns**, with their long pointed wings, resemble gulls but have thinner bodies and bills. If you spot terns circling noisily above your head, you're probably too close to their nesting area. Head quickly toward the water before the mother tern mounts an attack.

9. If you turn left toward Wasque Point and stroll for twenty minutes, you will land at the spot where people fish for "big blues." Bluefish and bass abound at Wasque Point due to the convergence of currents flowing toward the east and south. Because of these strong currents, swimming is prohibited here.

Erosion

If you look west toward Edgartown, you'll discover that Chappaquiddick is now really an island. Chappaquiddick has been an island only eleven times in the last 200 years when violent storms created a breach in the barrier beach connecting Chappaquiddick and Edgartown.

The section of sand bordering Katama Bay is a good example of up-island loss becoming down-island gain. Although erosion annually sweeps away about 8 feet of the Vineyard's southern shoreline, strong easterly currents have carried the sand from up-island cliffs and beaches to create this barrier beach.

You may spot sandpipers, tiny birds with long bills, which prefer isolated beaches where they peacefully can chase each receding wave in their quest for sand fleas. And the sand fleas, or "beach hoppers," emerge from their minuscule holes in the wet sand with their own mission: to find and gobble up plankton before the next wave rolls in.

Sandpiper

The boardwalk to Wasque Beach.

On a clear day looking out into the ocean at Wasque Point reveals a small sandy island, appropriately named Seal Island as it is home to a colony of seals. Swimmers along the south coast frequently see the seals frolicking in the water close to shore. If you travel north 2 miles from Wasque Point, you will enter Cape Poge Wildlife Refuge, a 509-acre property, also owned by The Trustees of Reservations. To reach Cape Poge, plan on hiking for several hours or you can try to hitch a ride on one of the four-wheel-drive vehicles heading to this secluded spot to sun, fish and swim. Driving on this sandy beach not only requires skill and practice but also a pricey permit sold by the Trustees. Another alternative is to explore Cape Poge via dune buggy on one of the Trustees' popular three-hour natural history tours.

The Cape Poge barrier beach was formed differently from other Vineyard barrier beaches. These south-facing beaches were formed when ocean currents carried sand and debris from the western end of the Vineyard. At east-facing Cape Poge, ocean tides, currents, and winds pulled glacial deposits from the ocean floor and created a sandbar that increased in height until it rose above sea level. This sandbar reduced the size and height of the waves that pounded the beach, allowing the barrier beach to grow to its present size.

Thousands of sea and shorebirds, including **ospreys**, **oystercatchers**, and **piping plovers** seek Cape Poge's isolated location to nest, feed, and rest. People who fish favor Cape Poge because the surf-casting off the refuge's outer shores has the reputation of being among the best on the Atlantic coast.

10. Upon reaching Wasque Point, turn left onto the wooden boardwalk.

11. After climbing the stairs, turn left on the trail, passing the reservation's premier picnic spot boasting many tables and benches and a great ocean view.

This section of the trail runs adjacent to Swan Pond before it converges with the path you walked earlier.

12. Upon reaching the boardwalk, turn right onto the access road that returns to the gatehouse and trailhead.

13. If you are biking and prefer to continue pedaling off-road, you can access one of the Land Bank's cross-island trails by returning to the path behind the gatehouse, and following it for 0.3 mile and then turning left onto the path with the Land Bank sign that leads to Poucha Pond Reservation.

Word of warning: Be careful as there may be thorns on these connector trails (I have gotten flat tires from them).

TRIP 7
CAMP MEETING GROUNDS

Location: Oak Bluffs
Rating: Easy
Distance: 1.3 miles
Restrooms: Public toilets are located in the Steamship Authority Terminal Building, located at the east end of Lake Avenue.
Food and Drink: Circuit Avenue, which flanks the east side of the Camp Meeting Grounds, offers a wide variety of shops and restaurants.
Fees: Cottage Museum, Flying Horses Carousel.

This walk will reveal remnants of the town's religious past.

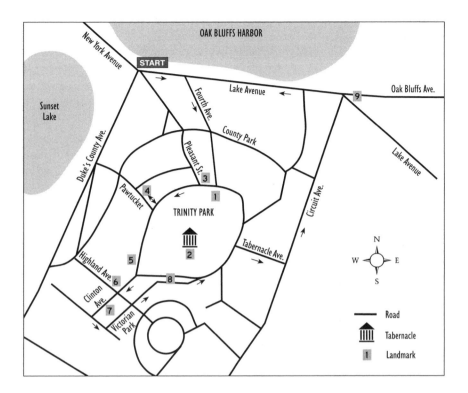

Directions

From the Steamship Authority Terminal on Sea View Avenue, proceed down Oak Bluffs Avenue to Lake Avenue. Bear right, remaining on Lake Avenue until you are standing in front of Oak Bluffs Harbor.

Trip Background

Now the liveliest island town, with the most nightclubs and fast food shops, ironically, Oak Bluffs originated as a place to pray, not play. In 1835, members of the Methodist Church began meeting in what was then known as Cottage City. Each August a small group pitched their tents in the campground, relaxed during the day, and attended nightly prayer meetings. Fifty years later, the town had turned into a full-fledged resort. To preserve their tightly-knit religious community with the church as its central focus, the Camp Meeting Association members built Victorian-era ornately trimmed, brightly colored homes, around the Tabernacle. Residents have conscientiously preserved these quaint cottages so visitors to the Camp Meeting Grounds can view the architecture as it was 150 years ago.

The Route

1. Begin on Lake Avenue, with the harbor on the left, and Sunset Lake on the right.

Originally, Sunset Lake and Oak Bluffs Harbor were one body of water, named Squash Meadow Pond. When the harbor and channel were dredged, Squash Meadow became a separate pond. The causeway, built between the pond and the harbor, further defined the separation.

Across from the harbor sits the **Wesley Hotel**, an example of the grand wooden hotels with large inviting verandas that have been popular for more than 150 years. Unfortunately, these structures often burned down. Originally constructed in 1879, the Wesley Hotel burned down in 1894. It was later rebuilt and today is the sole surviving Victorian-era hotel.

2. From the harbor, cross Lake Avenue on the crosswalk toward the Wesley Hotel. Climb the stairs on the left side of the hotel and enter the Camp Meeting Grounds. You'll see a sign for the Cottage Museum.

3. Proceed up Fourth Avenue. Note the house on the right, a good example of two small houses that were joined to make one.

4. Continue up Fourth Avenue, passing the One Way, Do Not Enter sign, following the signs to the Cottage Museum.

Note the care and attention paid to these colorful homes. Just the use of paint in an ocean community is a labor of love, as salt water causes paint to peel. Many owners have to paint or wash their houses each year. That's why in other locations on Martha's Vineyard you'll see mostly gray cedar-shingled homes.

5. Once you reach Trinity Park look straight ahead at the **Trinity Methodist Church,** designed as a miniature wooden Gothic cathedral (number 1 on the map). It was built in 1878 for use by the Association in summer and as a Methodist church in winter. Just behind the church in the center of the Campground stands the **Tabernacle** (2).

In 1879, Camp Meeting participants built the Tabernacle so their expanding population would have a suitable place to hold services. This wrought-iron structure replaced a one-ton canvas tent, which had replaced the original oak trees. Originally designed to be wood, the tabernacle was constructed out of iron because it was half the cost. The Tabernacle now seats more than 3,000 people and is used for interdenominational services and musical events.

6. Turn right to circle the Tabernacle.

Two Victorian-style cottages connected by their front porches.

In 1860, there were 500 tents in this area. Three hundred and fifteen small cottages, constructed between 1862 and 1880, replaced the tents. Each house had a wide double door, similar to the openings in the tents. Another double door on the second floor opened onto a cantilevered balcony. These upper-floor doors served two important purposes: they provided ventilation for the hot, stuffy second floor as well as allowing access for the beds and bureaus too large for the narrow stairway. Most of these original houses contained only four rooms: two bedrooms upstairs and a living room and bedroom downstairs. At that time there was no need for a kitchen or bathroom because there was no plumbing. All the cooking was done in cook tents. Note that all the homes have front porches that face the Tabernacle. Look above the front door to discover the year each cottage was built.

Another unusual sight (3) is on the corner of Pleasant Street: a lot with flowers, bushes and trees, but no cottage. Three homes once stood on this land but all were bought by the resident living in the house on the left, who gardens this plot. Many of the larger homes were constructed by combining two or three cottages.

Each housing lot is leased annually from the Association. The directors of the association have the option of not renewing the leases of tenants who do not keep their homes in good repair or who are too noisy. When these homes were first built they had neither foundations nor utilities, so an owner could easily move a house to a different location in the campground or to another area of Oak Bluffs.

As you walk, you'll notice that most of the cottages have the same general design: high peaked roofs, wide front porches, and a balcony over the front door. To individualize a cottage, an owner often used the newly invented jig-saw to cut elaborate filigree work painted with bright color combinations. A house with a radically different design can be found on the far right corner of Pawtucket Avenue (4). Its name, "Tall Timbers," is derived from the one-piece pine boards that start at the ground floor and travel up to the third story.

Continue to circle the Tabernacle until you reach number 10, a large home with the name The Ark (5) near the front door. This home, the largest and fanciest of that time, cost $3,500 to build. It belonged to William Sprague, the governor of Rhode Island during the Civil War.

7. Six houses down from The Ark, the walkway bears right. On the corner the **Cottage Museum** (6) invites the public to inspect the inside of a typical campground cottage to see how folks lived in the mid-1800s. The museum is open from 10 A.M. to 4 P.M. Monday through Saturday and 12 P.M. to 4 P.M. on Sunday. The fee for adults is $2.00 and children under 12 may enter for free.

8. From the museum, proceed straight onto Clinton Avenue. In this section, each house has more land and a grassy strip runs up the middle of the road. Four wealthy families from Brooklyn, N.Y., built cottages here in 1868. These "New York" cottages were elegantly furnished and had distinctive architectural features such as fancy moldings, along with brackets on the roof and over the doors. On the left side sits the Bishop Gilbert Haven Cottage where President Grant stayed in 1874. (7)

9. Continue down Clinton Ave until you reach an intersection. Turn left.

10. Take the next left onto Victorian Park to return to Trinity Park. On this street you'll notice that the homes are half the size of the ones on Clinton.

11. Turn left on Jordan Crossing.

12. Turn right at the stop sign to return to Trinity Park.

Instead of walking on the main road, take the side path with houses numbered in the 70s. Follow the narrow path until you reach number 70. As the small sign states, its name is Lawton Cottage (8) and in 1864 it was one of the first homes built here. The home was prefabricated but had to be taken apart and put on a sailing ship in Warren, R.I. Upon landing, the parts were hauled to this location and put back together.

13. Proceed back to Trinity Park. You may have noticed that the homes on the south side of the Tabernacle are considerably smaller than the ones on the north side. The north side is the preferred and more costly location as the front of the house gets the afternoon sun.

Continue to walk around the Campground and look at these colorful dwellings, representative of Carpenter Gothic architecture.

These homes are literally spotlighted during Illumination Night, usually held the third week in August (the date varies and is not advertised until the last minute in order to minimize the crowds). Each cottage, illuminated by ornate colorful Japanese-style lanterns, tries to outdo its neighbors in the number and variety of its lights. Throngs of viewers parade by on the sidewalks, while the cottage owners and their friends party on front porches and gaze at the spectators strolling by.

Illumination Night began in 1869 as an annual celebration of the end of the summer religious meetings. Its original name, Governor's Day, was in honor of the Governor who attended the event. The recent addition of a sing-along band concert has made this unique event even more festive.

14. Take your second right onto Tabernacle Avenue to Circuit Avenue. Just to the right, on Circuit Avenue, is the Secret Garden, a shop that specializes in books about the Vineyard and other memorabilia. Across the street is Craftworks, a gallery devoted to hand-made crafts.

15. Turn left. Walk on the right side of the street if you are looking for food or drink: Skinny's Fat Sandwiches, Ben and Bill's Chocolate Emporium, or Mad Martha's for ice cream.

This street has always been the main one in town. The Oak Bluffs Land and Wharf Company was formed in 1866 with the intention of turning Oak Bluffs into a summer resort. The Company designed most of the town and built their first commercial building, the Arcade, across the street from Ben and Bill's.

If you hunger for pizza or fried fish, continue down Circuit Ave to Giordano's, located on the corner of Circuit Avenue across from the Information Booth.

Across from Giordano's, on Lake Avenue, sits the oldest operating platform carousel in the country. The **Flying Horses** (9), built in 1876 and moved from Coney Island, NY, is registered as a National Historical Landmark. Riders on the original wooden horses continue the tradition of reaching for the brass ring in order to win a free ride. The carousel is open daily from 1 P.M. to 9 P.M. from May to November.

16. To return to your starting point, go west on Lake Avenue.

Religion's Influence on Oak Bluffs

Some speculate whether Martha's Vineyard would have developed into a popular resort if Oak Bluffs had not been the site of religious meetings. It is hard to believe that a beautiful island located near New York and Boston would remain a farming and fishing community. But it took the religious fervor of the island's summer visitors to jump-start the habit of annual pilgrimages to Cottage City, Oak Bluffs' name during its formative years.

This resurgence of religion began in the early nineteenth century when proponents of the Methodist movement, who preached personal salvation, were vigorously seeking converts. These preachers found outdoor camp meetings, which encouraged soul-searching and emotionalism, to be well-suited for this type of proseletyzing. In search of a meeting place, Jeremiah Pease of Edgartown sought a remote, undeveloped area near the seashore. He found a secluded spot under a large grove of oaks near Squash Meadow Pond. In the summer of 1835 the Methodists pitched their tents and established the Martha's Vineyard Camp Meeting. They called the area, now known as Trinity Park, Wesleyan Grove.

For many summers, church groups from Providence, New Bedford, Boston, and Nantucket attended meetings held under tall oak trees. Worshippers sat on rough benches and slept in society tents furnished only with blankets and straw that had canvas dividers to separate the sexes. As the camp meetings became more family oriented, families set up their own tents near their church tents.

The congregants found their annual Camp Meeting so pleasurable that they began to arrive earlier and remain later. In 1860 the Camp Meeting had grown to 500 tents with as many as 12,000 people attending Sunday services, and it adopted a new name, the Martha's Vineyard Camp Meeting Association. During this period, members built small Victorian-style cottages, similar to those popular in Newport, R.I., to replace their tents. The pervading spirit of gaiety was evident in the choice of color and architectural decoration of these homes. Although many of the houses have been remodeled and enlarged, their gingerbread trim and colorful facades continue to reflect the festive spirit of that time. However, the picket fence that was once built around the property to separate this religious community from those people who came to Oak Bluffs solely for recreational purposes has been taken down.

TRIP 8
TRADE WIND FIELDS PRESERVE

Location: Oak Bluffs
Rating: Easy
Distance: 1.5 miles (3 miles with the Farm Pond extension).

Enjoyable for dogs, dog-walkers, and off-road bikers, this trip also offers the opportunity to pick blueberries and huckleberries.

Directions
The preserve sits on County Road in Oak Bluffs, 1.7 miles north of the intersection with the Edgartown-Vineyard Haven Road and 0.5 mile south of the intersection with Wing Road. A dirt road leads to a large parking lot.

Trip Description
Take a wide grassy airplane landing field and surround it with woods and a scenic golf course. What do you get? A paradise for dogs and dog walkers. Dogs love the open grassland for chasing balls and each other. Walkers are grateful for the wide level paths that snake through woodlands and border the manicured Farm Neck Golf Club. The Farm Pond extension is a great way for off-road bikers to cycle to Oak Bluffs Center.

The Route

1. From the center of the parking lot proceed straight to the entrance path, located between two blue Handicapped Parking signs. The trailhead is marked by a Grass Airstrip 400 Yards sign and a Land Bank signboard.

2. Proceed on this wide level path surrounded by a typical Vineyard woodland, pine trees above with an understory of huckleberry bushes, until you come to a path on your left. Turn left.

Except for this green-blazed universal access path, all the other trails are marked with blue blazes.

3. Continue on this path until you reach the grassy airfield. Turn left and follow the path around the airfield.

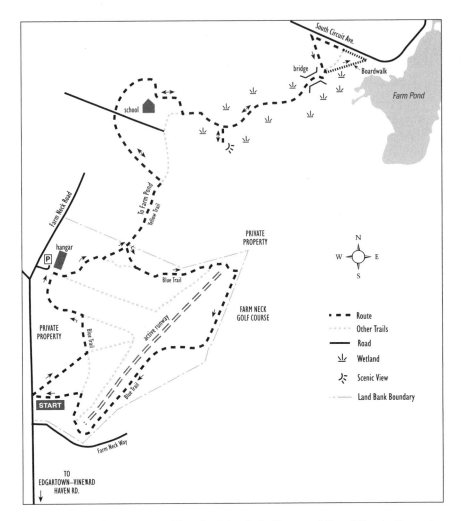

Owned and maintained by the Martha's Vineyard Land Bank Commission, Trade Wind Fields continues to be used as a grass-strip airport (pilots must have a "permission-to-land" slip issued by the Land Bank). For decades the land was mowed and rolled to ensure a smooth landing. As a result, half of the 72-acre preserve has remained sandplain grassland.

This habitat originally was formed when sand and gravel flowed off the melting glacier and formed much of Martha's Vineyard. Most of the sandplain, left unattended, became woodland (the State Forest is a good example). Sandplain soil is porous and supports only drought-resistant plants. Nantucket shadbush, bushy rock rose, and sandplain blue-eyed grass are several rare species that have adapted to this environment.

4. This path intersects with another. Bear right, continuing to walk alongside the airfield for about 100 feet and then turn left.

The trail first passes through a meadow before it heads into a pine forest. The meadow is host to a wide variety of wildflowers. In August white blooms from **pearly everlasting** dot the field. Its name describes its naturally dry blooms, which have a papery texture and last much longer than other flowers. The name **Queen Anne's Lace** accurately describes the lacey-looking clusters of tiny white flowers, often with one dark reddish-brown flower in the center, that grow all over the meadow. Later in the month, **golden asters**, whose small, bright yellow flowers form clusters at the end of their branches, brighten up the field.

Upon entering the forest, the path, cushioned with pine needles, passes oak saplings and an abundance of blueberry and huckleberry bushes. Before you start picking, check to make sure there is no poison ivy growing near the bushes.

5. If you wish to extend your walk by 1.6 miles, you can take the side path on the left to picturesque Farm Pond, another property owned by the Land Bank. If you prefer to remain in Trade Wind Fields, skip to No. 9.

6. Proceed straight on the path with yellow markers. When you reach a dirt road, turn left and then make a quick right onto the continuation of the path.

The path passes the modern Oak Bluffs Elementary School and its playing fields.

7. Follow the path as it crosses a meadow. A spur on the right leads to a boardwalk that extends out over a marsh, which slowly is drying up.

8. Continue 0.25 mile to Farm Pond and at the fork bear right. You can take a breather on the bench and admire this pristine pond before continuing on the boardwalk that runs beside the water.

During summer, Farm Pond has two very visible visitors: metal sculptures of the sea serpent Vanessa and her child perched in the center of the pond.

Queen Anne's lace

Low bush blueberry

Butterfly weed

9. Continue on the path to South Circuit Avenue. Turn left.

10. After about 200 feet, turn left onto the entrance path to Farm Pond.

11. To return, turn right onto the same path you just have walked.

12. To find the trail back to Trade Wind Fields from the Oak Bluffs School, turn left onto the dirt road and then take an immediate right onto the path.

13. Remain on the path for 0.3 mile and turn left onto the yellow blazed trail.

14. Turn left again to resume walking on the Blue Trail.

15. Follow the trail as it leaves the woods and runs beside the landing field. Turn left to continue your loop around the runway.

Although the airfield does not receive much traffic, be alert for the occasional plane landing or taking off. If you are walking a dog, make sure the dog is on a leash if a plane is taxiing. I've seen several dogs chase planes.

16. Turn right at the road that runs between the Farm Neck Golf Club and the air field.

Don't miss the fields of multicolored wildflowers growing among manicured putting greens and sand traps. Also leash your dog as many love to chase golf carts (including my dog)!

Remain on the dirt road as it reenters the grassland habitat. **Blueberry bushes** dot the grassland.

As you walk, you may hear the *thwunk* of tennis rackets hitting balls. The sounds come from tennis courts belonging to Farm Neck Golf Course.

The bright orange flower that adorns the field in August is called **butterfly weed**. It also is called pleurisy root because American Indians chewed on its root to alleviate the condition we now know as pleurisy. Watch for the monarch butterfly that often dines on its petals. Here again you'll find **Queen Anne's lace,** the tall flower that looks like its petals are made of white lace.

As you circle around the field, make sure that your dog stays on the trail, as planes land and take off in this section of the airfield.

17. Look on your left for a path through a split rail fence. Turn left onto that trail, heading into a pine forest.

18. Take your next left to return to the parking lot.

TRIP 9
CEDAR TREE NECK WILDLIFE SANCTUARY

Location: West Tisbury
Rating: Moderate
Distance: 2.8 miles
Food and Drink: Up-Island Cronig's Market and Fella's take-out, at
the intersection of State Road and Indian Hill Road.

**With its variety of terrain and dazzling views, Cedar Tree
Neck Wildlife Sanctuary is one of my favorite hiking spots on
Martha's Vineyard.**

Directions
Traveling west on State Road in West Tisbury, turn right on Indian Hill Road
(just past the turn to lower Lambert's Cove Road). Follow Indian Hill Road
for 1.3 miles. Turn right on Obed Daggett Road. Keep your eye out for the
Sanctuary signs as you remain on this dirt road for 1 mile.

Trip Description
Three separate trails provide a microcosm of the Vineyard's natural features
as they ramble through woods, across streams, by ponds, along a beach and
up to a bluff for a panoramic view of Vineyard Sound and the Elizabeth Islands. As a counterpoint to all this beauty, a sphagnum bog provides a smelly
diversion.

The Route
Watch for poison ivy in and around the trail (three shiny, dark-green leaflets). If you think you may have rubbed against the plant, scrub the area with
soap and water upon your return.

1. Facing the sanctuary from the parking lot, head to the left onto the White
Trail. The path is also named the Bruce Irons Trail, in memory of Irons, who
died in 1988. Irons loved kids, nature, and the Vineyard.

After walking for a few minutes on the white-blazed trail, look for a cluster
of **sassafras** trees, on both sides of the path. Sassafras trees have three different shapes of leaves: one, a simple oval shape; another, with two lobes that

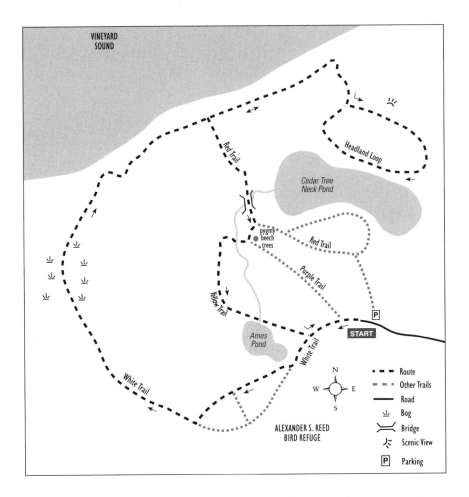

looks like a mitten; and a third, which has three lobes. Island settlers hollowed out sassafras trees to use as canoes and then boiled the roots and bark for tea.

Continue walking past the Purple Trail marker on the right. Look to your left at what used to be a forest of **red pine** trees. Hot, humid summers on Martha's Vineyard stressed the red pines, which grow best in a cool dry climate. They succumbed to the fungus, *Diplodia pinea*, and died.

2. Remain on the White Trail past the Yellow Trail marker on the right. Continue straight at the junction past the side path on the left that climbs to a glacial erratic and the Alexander S. Reed Bird Refuge.

Massachusetts ferns thrive in swampy areas. You can recognize a Massachusetts fern by its large leaves growing from one root stock and the downward slant of their lowest pair of leaflets.

The trail ascends and descends for about 0.5 mile until it reaches a wooden plank bridge that crosses a **sphagnum bog**. The odor comes from the release of sulfur from waterlogged soil.

This sphagnum bog began as a glacial excavation where water collected. Since water cannot flow out of this low-lying area and there are no underground streams to provide additional water, it just sits there. Because there is no water flow, there is little oxygen, which is necessary for decaying and composting to occur, so organisms that die in the bog decay very slowly. The sphagnum, one of the few plants that can grow in boggy areas with little oxygen, secretes acids that inhibit bacterial action. As a result, a bog is a good resource for archaeologists to discover what was living in this region thousands of years ago. In addition to its aid to scientific study, sphagnum moss is also useful in gardens for keeping the soil loose and retaining moisture.

As the trail descends to the beach, the trees become more stunted and deformed—the result of strong winds that bombard this exposed ridge.

3. Upon reaching the beach's rocky shore, turn right.

Look across Vineyard Sound toward the **Elizabeth Islands**. Naushon, the island directly ahead, is the largest of the chain. To the far left lies Cuttyhunk, which contains the town of Gosnold, the governmental center of the Elizabeth Islands. The other islands are privately owned.

4. Continue past the roped-off dune restoration area, one Red Trail marker, and more roped-off sections. After walking approximately 10 minutes, you'll reach a sign announcing the entrance to the Headland Loop. Turn right.

On your left you'll find typical beach vegetation, including ***Rosa rugosa***, bayberry and pasture rose, as well as the ubiquitous poison ivy. In summer *Rosa rugosa* sports a rose-colored flower, and in fall the flower turns into a large, red rose hip. **Pasture rose** displays a pink flower and five to nine small egg-shaped leaflets. **Bayberry** is a green shrub with many branches covered with small oblong leaves. If you crush its leaves, the distinctive bayberry aroma fills the air. In late summer and fall the female bayberry develops small, round, hard white berries, which are actually wax-covered nutlets. This waxy coating is used in making candles. So many grape vines grow here that it's easy to figure out how the island got its name.

5. Bear left at the fork.

6. On your ascent, step into the cleared lookout for a panorama, including the Elizabeth Islands straight ahead and the flickering beam of the Gay Head Lighthouse to the west.

Sassafras   *Bayberry*   *Beach pea*

As the trail veers inland, the vegetation changes and you will find your-self under a cooling canopy formed by the arching branches of **sassafras** and **tupelo** trees.

7. The trail descends between **grape vines** and bayberry bushes to the beach. Turn left to walk back beside the roped-off dunes to the Red Trail.

8. Turn left onto the Red Trail back into the sanctuary.

Before you go inland, look down at the **beach grass**. Avoid walking on this plant. Crushing it hinders the grass from performing a most important function: stabilizing dune areas to prevent erosion. Beach grass provides a wonderful lesson in adaptation. It can survive in hot dry locations because the grass curls to avoid drying out. Feel the grass's rough edges and you will know why animals are not inclined to nibble on it. **Beach pea** grows amid the beach grass. In spring it produces purple, pea-shaped flowers which in summer are replaced by pods.

On your left is a great view of Cedar Tree Neck Pond.

9. Continue straight past stunted oak trees, cross a plank bridge and turn right onto the Yellow Trail.

Keep your eye out on the left side of the trail for a grove of Cedar Tree Neck's famous **bonsai** (pygmy) **beech trees**. These hundred-year-old trees normally would have grown to a height of 80 feet, but their exposed loca-tion, where they are regularly blasted by salt-laden wind, prevented them from growing tall. Their wide trunks attest to their age, but their angular horizontal branches have been shaped by fierce wintery gales.

10. Bear right, remaining on the Yellow/Irons Trail as it makes two stream crossings.

Sensitive ferns, sturdy ferns with broad, almost triangular leaves, line the bank at the second stream crossing.

Bonsai (pygmy) beech trees.

The #6 marker refers to the two streams which join here. The larger stream empties into Cedar Tree Neck Pond where the water then travels underground into the ocean.

The #5 marker on the right refers to the stand of **beech trees** growing in this section. Beech trees grow best in protected areas where the soil retains moisture. Cedar Tree Neck is one of the few places on the island with these conditions, so beech trees grow throughout the sanctuary.

There are three major reasons why beech trees dominate an area: First, beech tree roots grow partially above ground so they don't leave much room for other plants to grow. Second, baby beech trees sprout from these roots and then get nourishment from the parent tree so they grow very quickly and again prevent other plants from growing. Third, the leaves of beech trees are acidic, so when they fall off the tree and decay they make the soil acidic, making it difficult for other plants to grow.

11. Just after passing the #5 marker, turn left, following the Yellow/Irons Trail to Ames Pond.

The bench overlooking the pond provides a wonderful vantage point for viewing the wildlife living there. Silvery-winged **dragonflies** and **damsel-flies** flit about, **tadpoles** swim along the bottom; tiny **water striders** scoot on top of the water while **whirligig beetles** run in circles. Turtles, geese, and miniscule frogs called **pinkletinks** often appear. If you are walking in spring and hear what sounds like a frenzied flock of starlings, you are listening to the high-pitched mating calls of male pinkletinks.

12. Continue on the Yellow Trail to the intersection with the White Trail. Turn left onto the White Trail to return to the parking lot.

TRIP 10
BLACKWATER POND RESERVATION
AND WOMPESKET PRESERVE

Location: West Tisbury
Rating: Easy
Distance: 3.5 miles

Take this trip for terrific hiking, scenic pond views, and berries for nibbling.

Directions
From the intersection of State Road and Lambert's Cove Road, proceed on Lambert's Cove Road for 1.8 miles. The reservation is on the left 0.5 mile from the Tisbury/West Tisbury town line sign. The reservation sign and map are on the west side of the parking lot.

Trip Description
The Martha's Vineyard Land Bank recently cut trails through Blackwater Pond Reservation and it's a fabulous addition to Vineyard conservation land. The paths wind around five different ponds, offering a variety of views. The reservation conveniently connects to Wompesket Preserve, a small but topographically interesting property that had been difficult to access.

The Route

1. From the parking lot, walk by Northern Duarte's Pond.

During one of my visits two young boys were fishing from the wharf. They already had caught six trout. I could not imagine how fish arrived at this land-locked pond. I later learned that each spring the pond is stocked

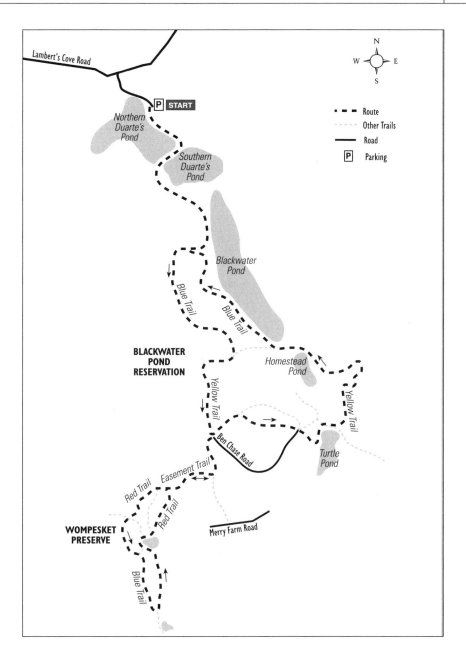

with trout in preparation for the annual Children's Fishing Derby. Boating is also allowed so you can bring your kayak, launch it from the dock, and paddle around.

The name of the neighboring body of water is Southern Duarte's Pond. Bright white lilies nestle in green lily pads from early morning until noon, at which time the blossoms close and only the lily pads are visible.

Among the vegetation that grow near the wooden plank benches that line the path beside the water are the small, multi-stemmed **chokecherry trees**, **wild indigo** with its tiny yellow pea-like flowers, **oxeye daisy** sporting white petals with yellow button centers, and **sensitive ferns** distinguished by their broad triangular leaves.

2. Cross the cedar-plank bridge onto the Land Bank Easement Trail (land owned by the Nature Conservancy) into the forest. The trail runs by a huge glacial **erratic**, a boulder left by the receding glacier about 15,000 years ago, and old stone walls, indicating that this land had once been farmed.

Proceed through an opening in the stone wall but be careful of **poison ivy** (clusters of three green leaves which are shiny if the ivy is growing in a sunny spot or dull if it is in the shade) growing on both sides of the trail.

3. After about 0.5 mile on the easement trail, you reach Blackwater Pond Reservation. At the T intersection, turn right toward Wompesket Preserve. Blue blazes are on the trees on both sides of the trail. Blueberry bushes line the path.

4. At the junction of the Yellow and Blue Trails (barricade in front), turn right onto the Yellow Trail.

5. Turn right at the next T-intersection and Eastern Loop Trail sign.

6. Make a quick left onto the easement trail to Wompesket Preserve.

7. Take your next right to enter Wompesket Preserve. There may not be a sign since you are entering through the "back door."

8. Take your next right onto the red-blazed trail loop that runs through a wetland environment with greenbrier growing all around. Sweet pepperbush, whose fragrant, white spiky flowers perfume the air, is commonly found in wetlands.

Wild indigo

Oxeye daisy

Russian olive

Lily pads on Southern Duarte's Pond.

9. Bear right, now walking on the blue-blazed trail through a meadow. When I was here in late August I saw many wildflowers: the bright red **cardinal flower**, lots of **goldenrod** and a cluster of dull pink flowers with the name **Joe-Pye weed**. The flower is named after Joe Pye, an American Indian who lived in New England in the late 1700s. He supposedly used this weed to cure fevers.

Many **Russian olive** trees grow here. An introduced species, this shrub, with its long slender leaves and silvery undersurfaces, has proliferated on the island.

10. After completing the blue-blazed loop, bear right, returning to the red-blazed wetland area.

11. At the end of the Red Trail, continue straight to return to Blackwater Pond Reservation.

12. At the V intersection, bear left, following the Trail Easement to Black-water Pond sign.

13. Upon reaching a road, turn right.

14. Immediately turn left onto the path that you walked earlier.

Remain on the path, following the Eastern Loop Trail and Ripley's Field signs, passing several handsome **eastern white pine** trees, distinguished from other pines by their blue-green needles in bundles of five.

15. At the Yellow Trail sign, cross two dirt roads to access a trail where you will pass by a bench and a cleared area revealing Turtle Pond.

16. Take the next right, following the directions on the sign: "Blackwater Trail system right and next left."

17. Turn left as directed and continue to follow the Eastern Loop yellow-blazed trail in the direction of Ripley's Field.

A **sassafras** sapling, as evidenced by its three different leaves, stands at the turn.

On your left lies Homestead Pond along with many **dangleberry bushes**. Dangleberries appear to be a cross between blueberries and huckleberries, given that they are blue like blueberries and have seeds in their centers like huckleberries, but they really are their own distinct shrub. They bear fruit later than huckleberries, have much longer stems than the other two, and are edible.

A boardwalk extends over a collection of dainty **marsh ferns** and huge **cinnamon ferns**, whose name is derived from its golden cinnamon color, which changes to bright green in summer. Both varieties prefer moist shady locations.

Nearing the end of our walk, Blackwater Pond finally appears. Continue straight, passing through a break in the stone wall.

18. At the fork, bear right onto the blue-blazed trail.

A viewing platform provides a view of marshy Blackwater Pond. Several years ago its dam broke and water flowed out. It will take several years for ten acres of water to refill and transform the bog back to a pond.

19. At the next intersection, bear right following the Trail Easement to Duarte's Pond sign.

On your second passing of the two Duarte's Ponds, listen for the deep croaking sounds of the **pickerel frogs** and watch for **eastern painted turtles**.

20. After crossing the boardwalk over the ponds, turn left to return to the parking area.

TRIP 11
LONG POINT WILDLIFE REFUGE

Location: West Tisbury

Rating: Easy: wide, level trails.

Distance: From the parking lot, along the beach, and to and through the trails: 2.5 miles.

Fees: $10.00 per car plus $3.00 for each adult. Members of The Trustees of Reservations and children under 15 may enter for free.

Restrooms: A portable toilet is set back east of the parking area and a regular toilet is located in the Visitor's Center near the walking trails.

You can jump the waves on the beach, swim in the pond, and hike the trails.

Directions

The summer entrance, open from 9 A.M. to 6 P.M., June 15 to September 15, can be reached via Waldron's Bottom Road on the south side of the Edgartown-West Tisbury Road 0.3 mile west of the airport entrance (second dirt road on the left after the airport). Proceed 1.3 miles on Waldron's Bottom Road, turn left, and then make a quick right on to Hughe's Thumb Road. Remain on this road for 1.2 miles to the gatehouse. When the parking lot is full, rangers post a sign at the turnoff from the Edgartown-West Tisbury Road.

The off-season entrance, via Deep Bottom Road, is 0.8 mile farther west than the summer entrance.

Trip Description

"No gain without pain" or "seek and ye shall finally find" describes an excursion to Long Point Wildlife Refuge, one of my favorite places on Martha's Vineyard. You can walk for miles along the coast and jump the waves, swim in the calm waters of Long Cove Pond, and explore the refuge's tranquil trails around the ponds and cove. Or you can hunt for blue-claw crabs and take a kayak tour in Tisbury Great Pond.

Be aware—their small parking lot fills quickly on a hot summer day. If you don't mind biking on unpaved roads, you never will be refused entry nor will you have to pay the $10.00 charge for autos.

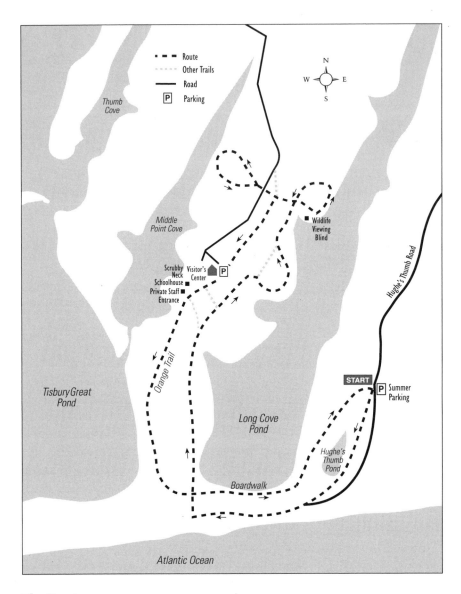

The Route

1. From the summer parking lot, proceed south to the ocean on the path that runs between Long Cove Pond on the right and Big Homer's Pond on the left.

The numerous small ponds and coves on the southern side of the island were originally created by streams from melting glacial ice. After the glacier disappeared, the streams dried up, leaving wide openings that filled with a mix of sea water and fresh water from underground springs. These coves and ponds continue to contain both fresh and salt water.

Note the vegetation that has adapted to this harsh ocean front environment. Don't get near the omnipresent **poison ivy**, which thrives in sunny arid areas. Near the dunes you'll find **beach pea** sprawled on the sand. In spring this ground-hugging plant produces a purple flower that turns into a pea pod in summer. In autumn, **seaside goldenrod** decorates the dunes with bright yellow flowers. **Dusty miller** is a bluish-gray plant with lacy leaves. Its dusty covering conserves water so that it can survive hot sunny summers. Be careful not to walk on the **beach grass,** which is essential for maintaining the fragile dunes. The grass preserves moisture in its long blades by curling inward to avoid the sun's drying rays.

2. Upon reaching the beach, turn right and walk past Long Cove Pond until you reach the next beach entrance.

3. From the beach turn right onto a path through the sandplain grassland, a rare landscape created by outwash from melting glaciers. Sand and gravel picked up by the glaciers as they moved southward more than 15,000 years ago were left behind when they melted, covering much of the southern side of the island.

At Long Point, the sandy soil, combined with strong winds and salt spray, determine which species can survive under such harsh conditions. Some of the rare plants that grow on this sandplain are Nantucket shadbush, bushy rockrose, and sandplain blue-eyed grass. Hundreds and thousands of years ago this prairie-like habitat was maintained by frequent fires that prevented vegetation overgrowth. In order to preserve Long Point, The Trustees of Reservations have instituted a system of controlled fires. They hope the fires will encourage the continued existence of endangered vegetation that has adapted to this sandplain.

Several species of rare birds inhabit this property including the **northern harrier**, a slender, narrow-winged hawk that you may spot soaring over the meadows and ponds. **Common** and **least terns**, white-bodied with black caps, patrol the beach and then dive into the ocean for fish. If you see a shore bird darting across the sand and then stopping suddenly and taking off, it probably is a variety of **plover**.

As you walk, you will see Long Cove Pond on your on your right and Tisbury Great Pond on your left.

4. Before you reach the building that houses the staff of Long Point, turn right onto a wide grassy trail.

5. To begin a scenic loop, bear right at the Exit sign into a forest filled with mini-oak trees, reduced in size by continual wind blasts. This path meanders through an oak woodland composed of four varieties of oak trees: white, black, scrub, and post. To identify **white oak**, look for leaves with five to nine rounded lobes. **Post oak** also has rounded lobes but usually has only five that form the shape of a cross. **Black oak** has lobes with bristly tips, while **scrub oak** also has leaves with five lobes and bristly tips, but its lobes aren't as deeply cut.

6. Turn right onto a side path to view the wildlife in Long Cove Pond.

7. Turn right at the fork to proceed to the second loop.

8. Bear right at the fork to enter the second Long Cove Pond Loop.

9. After exploring the second loop, turn right and make a quick left to then cross the off-season access road and proceed to another loop trail that skirts Middle Point Cove.

10. Bear right at the fork to begin the Middle Point Cove Loop. Because this section is more protected, the oak trees have grown to a normal size.

11. After exploring the loop, turn right onto a trail that travels through a heavily wooded area filled large oaks and **bracken ferns,** which have three leaves growing from a single stalk.

12. Cross the road again and take the first right, which leads to the off-season parking lot.

13. At the parking lot, turn right to pick up the path that runs through the middle of the lot.

14. Follow this path to the Visitor Center.

15. Turn left on the road that runs by Middle Point Cove and then leads to a path that borders Tisbury Great Pond.

Common tern

White oak

Post oak

16. To walk along the pond's shore, follow the trail until it veers close to the pond; turn right onto a steep boat slide that leads to the water.

The water level in Tisbury Great Pond depends on whether there is an opening in the barrier beach that separates it from the ocean. Often storms produce a breach, but if there have been no storms, an opening is dug twice a year to allow the ocean to flow through to cleanse the pond and maintain its brackish quality.

Be careful of the shellfish that inhabit the pond. Tisbury Great Pond is seeded for oysters whose razor-sharp shells can cut the feet of unwary walkers. Severed pincers of blue-claw crabs collect on the sand, but it's the unsevered ones that you should avoid. Low tide draws net-swishing crab-collectors trying to capture the wily crustaceans.

17. After your pond walk return to the trail.

18. Turn right on the Orange Trail to walk toward the beach.

19. The path swings around and meets the trail to Long Cove Pond. Turn left at the sign to walk on the boardwalk bordering Long Cove Pond.

20. When the boardwalk ends, continue walking beside Long Cove Pond until you reach the path that returns to the parking area.

TRIP 12
SEPIESSA POINT RESERVATION

Location: West Tisbury

Rating: Easy

Distance: 2.5 miles

Food and Drink: The closest spot is Alley's General Store and Back Alley Café 0.4 mile west of the intersection of New Lane and the Edgartown/West Tisbury Road.

Restroom: At the boat launch parking area.

Shaded trails and an opportunity for a swim in Tisbury Great Pond makes this a perfect hike for a hot summer day.

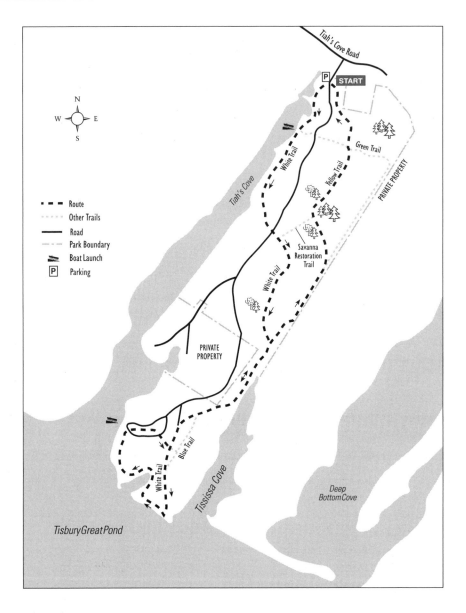

Directions

On the Edgartown-West Tisbury Road, proceed 2.5 miles west of the intersection with Barnes Road. Turn left onto New Lane (Pondview Farm sign at the turn). Follow New Lane for 1.2 miles. Turn right onto a dirt road that leads to the reservation.

Huckleberry   *Osprey*   *Shadbush*

Trip Description

What makes Sepiessa Point Reservation such a great destination on a hot summer day? Its location on Tisbury Great Pond. After biking or hiking on shady, wide, well-maintained paths to scenic Sepiessa Point, you can peel off your clothes and go for a swim at the half-mile-long sandy beach. Bring beach shoes; because the pond is seeded for oysters, sharp shells are scattered along the beach and in the water. The Land Bank has created a boat launching area so you also have the option of paddling in and out of coves or sailing and windsurfing on the pond (Trip 42).

The Route

1. From the parking lot, proceed straight on the White Trail, which borders Tiah's Cove. Follow the trail as it passes a boat launch site, continues straight for 0.3 mile and then bears left, crosses a dirt road, and enters a pitch pine forest.

2. Bear right on the White Trail, passing the Savanna Restoration Trail on the left.

3. After walking through a woodland of **scrub oak** trees and **huckleberry bushes,** turn right, remaining on the White Trail.

The path heads toward Tississa Cove. The clearings near the pond allow a full view of the red barn on the other side.

Watch for the eagle-like **osprey** that may be perching on a pole at the southern tip of the farm or plunging feet-first into the water in search of fish.

As the trail approaches Tisbury Great Pond, the trees become smaller and the vegetation sparser due to the wind and salt spray. Growing in this sunny sandplain section are plants that usually are not found on the mainland such as **sandplain flax**, **nantucket shadbush**, and **bushy rock rose**. The **caribou moss** growing along the trail is further evidence of the harsh climatic conditions in this area.

From the trail, a view across Tississa Cove.

4. The path merges with a carriage road. Bear left, heading toward the pond. A side trail, blazed blue, leads to the parking area for the boat launch, beach, and portable toilet.

You can go straight to the shore to swim or walk along the beach to the boat launch area. If you prefer to continue hiking, take the blue-blazed side trail.

The oyster shells scattered on the sand are the result of oyster seeding in the pond. Since oysters require salt water to breed, twice a year a breach is created in the barrier beach to allow the ocean to flow through to the pond. If you visit Sepiessa Point soon after the breach was dug, you'll find a much wider beach as the water level in the pond recedes significantly.

Blue-claw crabs also inhabit Tisbury Great Pond. During low tide you may see waders armed with nets attempting to scoop up the fast-moving crustaceans.

As you walk along the beach, you may spot several of the ten coves and ponds that extend out from Tisbury Great Pond like fingers on a hand, with Black Point Pond forming the thumb. These ponds and coves make up a series that span the southern side of Martha's Vineyard and are separated from the Atlantic Ocean by thin strips of barrier beaches.

To the left lies **Long Point Wildlife Refuge** (Trip 11).

5. To return, you can either retrace your route on the White Trail or if you have walked along the beach to the boat launch site, take a right toward the dirt road and pick up the trail across from the boat launch access road.

6. Cross the road onto the Blue Trail. The sign reads Trail to Point.

7. Now back at the White Trail, turn left, following the sign to Inland Trails and Upper Trailheads.

8. At the junction with the Yellow Trail, bear right onto the Yellow Trail.

9. Follow the Yellow Trail until you reach the Savanna Restoration sign. Turn left.

The Martha's Vineyard Land Bank is restoring this section in order to attract hawks and owls. Owls tend to be more active when it's dark but you may spot the rare **northern harrier**, a marsh hawk around 2 feet long that often glides close to the ground searching for prey. The males are pale grey and the females are brown.

10. Take the next right, remaining on the Yellow Trail, to return to the entrance.

Fighting for Public Access

The public has fought over access to Tisbury Great Pond since 1674, when Simon Athearn purchased the surrounding land from an American Indian named Jude without getting permission from Thomas Mayhew, the lord proprietor of the island. Even though Massachusetts law mandates public use of large ponds, Tisbury Great Pond was surrounded by private land so there was no public road to the water until 1991. Before tourists arrived on Martha's Vineyard, informal access was granted to people who wanted to fish. In exchange, they presented consenting landowners with a portion of their catch.

As tax assessments increased and parcels of land were subdivided, informal access became more difficult. In an attempt to gain public access to the pond, the town of West Tisbury approached every landowner along the pond. No one was interested in selling until January 1991 when the McAlpin family let it be known that they wished to sell their entire 165-acre property. In May 1991, the property was purchased for $1,925,000 by the Martha's Vineyard Land Bank, a conservation organization, which is funded by a 2 percent tax on real estate transfers. One of the main reasons for the Land Bank's purchase of Sepiessa Point was to allow community access to Tisbury Great Pond.

TRIP 13
MIDDLE ROAD SANCTUARY

Location: Chilmark
Rating: Moderate: a long gradual climb
Distance: 2.7 miles
Food and Drink: The closest shops are in Chilmark Center, just
west of the junction of Middle Road and South Road (2.3
miles). The Chilmark Store is known for its pizza, and Chilmark
Chocolates for—you guessed it—its chocolate.

This tranquil hike ascends through an oak forest with an understory of blueberry and huckleberry bushes.

Directions
From the intersection of Middle Road and Music Street in West Tisbury,
proceed 2.1 miles on Middle Road. The parking lot and sanctuary are on the
left (soon after passing Tea Lane on the right).

Trip Description
My favorite time to hike through Middle Road Sanctuary is mid-summer,
when blueberries and huckleberries are at their peak. Oak trees provide
shade as I nibble succulent berries and climb the trail that overlooks the
south coast and Chilmark Pond. I compete for berries with a wide variety of
birds that inhabit the sanctuary, including great-crested flycatchers, downy
and hairy woodpeckers, red-tailed hawks, white breasted nuthatches, rufous-sided towhees, Carolina wrens, and chickadees.

The Route

1. From the parking lot, head onto the trail.
The Sheriff's Meadow Foundation owns and manages this 110-acre sanctuary. For more than 35 years, the Sheriff's Meadow Foundation has acquired and received more than 2000 acres of land on Martha's Vineyard.
Some of these properties are protected land and are not open to the public.
Others, like Middle Road Sanctuary, provide visitors with the opportunity
for a relaxing hike through varied island terrain. The name "sanctuary" de-

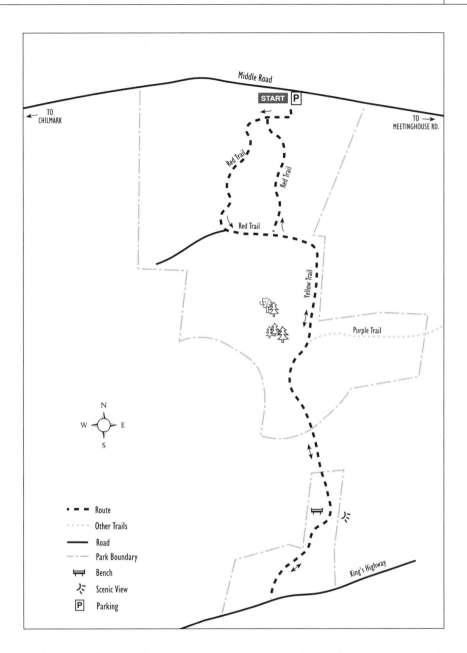

scribes how the foundation wants its property to be used: communing with nature is fine, but neither biking, picnicking, nor camping is allowed. However, there are no rules prohibiting berry-picking!

2. At the fork, bear right onto the beginning of the Red Trail.

This trail loops around through the usual Vineyard woodland: black, white and scarlet oak trees above with an under layer of **huckleberry**, **blueberry**, **dangleberry**, and **bayberry** bushes.

The huckleberry, blueberry, and dangleberry bushes have similar small, green, oval leaves. However, their berries differ, although all are equally tasty. The huckleberry, which predominates in this sanctuary, is black and contains a tiny seed that crunches when chewed. The blueberry is blue with a powdery surface. The dangleberry appears as a cross between the two with a blue powdery surface surrounding a tiny crunchy seed. The inedible bayberry has a larger oval leaf and when crushed gives off the fragrant bayberry scent. Its small, round, hard white berries, attached to the base of the stem, fortify birds during winter.

3. Turn left onto what used to be an old carriage road, remaining on the Red Trail.

4. At the triangular intersection, leave the old road at the Walkers Only sign, continuing on the Red Trail.

5. Proceed straight onto the mile-long Yellow Trail.

This route ascends to the peak and winds through more diverse vegetation, courtesy of the clay soil that holds water closer to the surface than on the sandier Red Trail. **Bracken ferns** and **cinnamon ferns** line the trail and **wild grape vines** climb over oak tree branches and viburnum bushes.

For a short distance the trail parallels a stone wall, which formerly served as a boundary line between the sheep farms that occupied this land.

6. Bear right at the intersection with the Purple Trail, remaining on the Yellow Trail

We have the last glacier to credit with the sanctuary's distinctive terrain. About 15,000 years ago, as the glacier inched its way southward, it finally stopped and began to melt at Middle Road Sanctuary (and the surrounding

Bracken ferns

Cinnamon fern

latitude). This last stopping point, called a terminal moraine, contains the characteristic steep ridges and valleys that resulted from glacial melting. Besides huckleberry bushes, the sanctuary boasts glacial erratics, boulders pulled from bedrock and then left behind when the glacier melted.

7. The path meets an unpaved road. Cross the road and look directly ahead for the Yellow Trail marker. Continue on the path that runs beside an old stone wall on the right.

After walking about 500 feet past the large house on the left, look on your right for a bench. Across the trail from the bench is a cleared section allowing a vista of Chilmark Pond and the Atlantic Ocean.

The gnarled branches of the low scrub oak trees result from winds that batter this peak.

The trail meanders through a heavily wooded section until it ends at an ancient dirt road named the King's Highway. If you turn left and follow King's Highway for almost 0.5 mile, you'll reach Meetinghouse Road, another old unpaved way. Another left turn and an additional 0.7 mile will return you to Middle Road. To get back to the sanctuary, turn left on Middle Road.

8. If you are returning via the same route, follow the Yellow Trail until it merges with the Red Trail.

9. Turn right onto the Red Trail to hike the remaining 0.3 mile to the entrance. Again, you'll hike through an oak woodland with an undergrowth of huckleberry bushes. Another large glacial erratic appears on the left.

TRIP 14
FULLING MILL BROOK PRESERVE

Location: Chilmark

Rating: Moderate. The first half of the walk is hilly; the return is on level ground.

Distance: 2.25 miles

Food and drink: The closest stores are in Chilmark Center, 1 mile west on Middle Road.

The route follows a gurgling brook that meanders through a forest bursting with bird songs.

Directions

Proceed southwest on Middle Road for 3 miles. Turn left onto Henry Hough Lane (the street after Fulling Mill Brook Road) and left again into the parking lot for cars and bicycles. The South Road entrance (1 mile west of Meetinghouse Road) also has a bike rack and parking for several cars.

Trip Description

Sound effects accompany you on this hike to one of my favorite picnic spots on Martha's Vineyard. The brook that runs through this property provides an ideal environment for vegetation that prefers lots of moisture. The boulder-lined bank of Fulling Mill Brook is a good place to eat your lunch. The post-lunch return rambles across meadows and through woodlands.

The Route

1. From the parking lot, walk behind the trail board onto the Green Trail where you will navigate your first brook crossing (easy, up the stairs and over the walkway). The boardwalk leads to a bridge where a bench awaits if you feel the need for a rest stop. The trail ascends before it meets a dirt road.

2. Cross the dirt road and continue onto a narrow path.

The trail passes a mossy glacial erratic, a boulder picked up by the glacier and then deposited 15,000 years ago when the glacier began to melt.

The path descends and crosses the Blue Trail.

A long, narrow bridge signals another brook crossing. Next, a steep incline ascends to the crest of a hill covered with grapevines and prickly greenbrier. The path descends to a tiny wood-plank bridge. Cutting across two old stone walls, the rocky trail ascends to the top of a hill. Look to your left for a clearing with a seascape of the south side of the island.

Another set of steep, narrow stairs leads to a rest stop with a bench overlooking the Fulling Mill Brook. This stop provides an excellent opportunity to inspect the vegetation growing in this moist area. Most ferns seek moisture. Among the varieties that grow here are marsh, Massachusetts, New York, and cinnamon. The thin, delicate **marsh fern** with lance-shaped leaves contrasts with the large, strong **cinnamon fern** that grows in clusters. Whereas the marsh fern prefers wet areas, the **New York fern** grows along drier edges of swamps and in sunny woodlands. You can distinguish the New York fern by looking for three or more leaves to a tuft. The **Massachusetts fern** looks very similar to the New York and marsh ferns but if you look closely at its leaflets, you'll find they are oblong rather than lance-shaped.

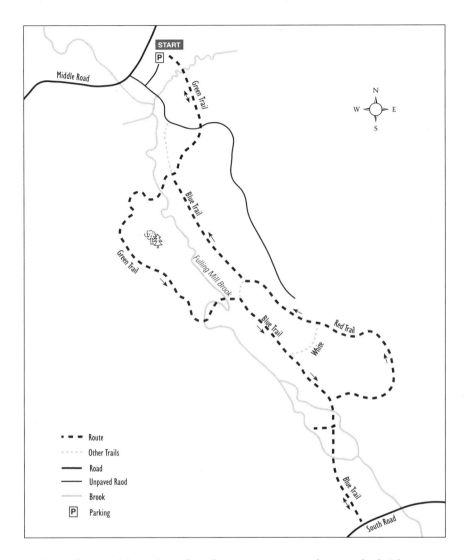

Sassafras and **American beech** trees grow near the river bed. It's easy to spot the sassafras tree. Look for leaves that have three distinct shapes, one with one lobe, another with two lobes that looks like a mitten, and the third with three lobes.

Tupelo trees also prefer a moist habitat. This species is easiest to spot in autumn when its small oval-shaped leaves turn bright orange and red. The tupelo tree also is called **black gum** and on Martha's Vineyard, **beetle-bung**.

A long narrow boardwalk crosses the brook. Right before the end of the boardwalk, look to your left at the **red (swamp) maple** tree bending across the river bank. Its stem bifurcates, one section growing horizontally, parallel to the boardwalk.

3. Turn right onto the Blue Trail, the old carriage lane that connects Middle and South Roads.

4. After walking for about 5 minutes, first entering a meadow, then a woodland, look on your right for the unmarked path that leads to the boulder-lined banks of the Fulling Mill Brook.

Large flat rocks line both sides of the brook and make perfect picnic tables. A tiny waterfall adds just the right sound effects. Although the water looks inviting, do not drink it. Please carry out your trash.

The name of this property was derived from the fulling mill located here from 1694 to 1770. "Fulling" is a term that refers to an early method of removing oil and grease from wool by using hydrated aluminum and magnesium silicate. At the fulling mill, workers first cleaned, shrunk, and thickened the wool. Running water from the brook propelled hammers that pounded these large pieces of wool until they became smooth enough to use for making clothes.

5. Return to the Blue Trail. If you wish, you can turn right to follow the carriage road to imposing stone columns at the main entrance to what used to be a gristmill. In 1850, the Tilton family, descendants of the owners of the fulling mill, used rushing water from the brook to rotate heavy stones which then ground grain.

Or you can retrace your route on the Blue Trail.

6. From the turn-off to the brook, returning on the Blue Trail, proceed about 0.2 mile.

Tupelo

New York fern

Resting and reading at a glacial erratic.

7. Turn right onto the Red Trail.

The dry woodlands and meadows along the Red Trail contrast with the lush wetlands bordering the Green Trail. Here the vegetation consists mainly of **black** and **white oaks** often with an understory of **bayberry bushes**, distinguished by their waxy, green leaves. An old maple tree with mottled bark and wide branches sits on the left side, providing shade and shelter for anyone in need of an excuse to stop and rest.

The trail passes the intersection with the White Trail, a spur that connects the Red and Blue trails.

8. The Red Trail cuts through a stone wall right before the T intersection with the Blue Trail. Turn right onto the Blue Trail. You can remain on the Blue Trail back to your starting point or proceed to No. 9.

9. Turn right onto the Green Trail and retrace your original route.

TRIP 15
PEAKED HILL RESERVATION

Location: Chilmark
Rating: Moderate: two steep hills.
Distance: 1.5 miles

Hike the second highest point on Martha's Vineyard for expansive views of the island and its surroundings.

Directions

At the intersection of Middle Road and Tabor House Road, go 0.5 mile on Tabor House Road and turn left, or from the intersection of North and Tabor House Roads go 0.5 mile and turn right (opposite the Chilmark landfill) onto a dirt road. Follow the road, turning right at each fork until you reach the entrance to the reservation. The entry road runs beside a sheep farm with lovely new stone walls built to replicate walls that farmers used to delineate their property and contain their livestock.

Trip Description

Mountain climbing on Martha's Vineyard? Well, not quite. Climbing to a 311-foot summit is as close as you are going to get. But the views from two different "peaks" do offer mountain-size views of the South Shore, Aquinnah, and the Elizabeth Islands. If you scale the peak in August, your reward will be bountiful blueberries and blackberries.

The Route

1. From the parking lot, head right onto the Blue Trail, also referred to as the Northern Loop.

In the mid-1980s the owners of 160 acres of land around the summit sold their properties for development. The developer obtained approval to build a subdivision, laid out the roads, and constructed the foundations. The 1990 recession prevented the developer from getting financing. When the property ended up in receivership and was auctioned, the Land Bank submitted the winning bid and transformed the roads into wide, level trails.

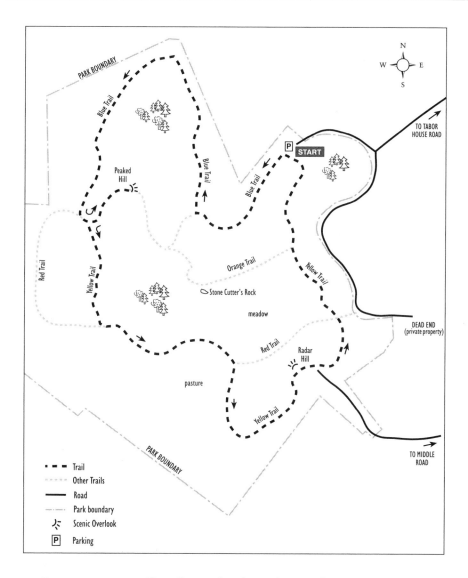

During summer, yellow flowers brighten the woodland: **black-eyed Susan** flaunts bright yellow petals and a black center, **stiff goldenrod** produces tall yellow flowers and **wild indigo** displays a delicate yellow pea-like flower. In August, be alert for juicy **blackberries**, protected by their prickly stems from hungry hikers.

About ten minutes into the walk, look for **hay-scented** and **bracken ferns** on both sides of the trail. The hay-scented fern has long, pale green fronds and is shaped like a Christmas tree, wide at the bottom and tapering to its tip. Its name is derived from the odor released when its fronds are crushed. The bracken fern is easily identified as its leaves always grow in clusters of three.

2. Take a right at the clearing, remaining on the Blue Trail.

If you are walking with children, point out the large oak on the left side of the trail. Its wide branches are perfect for climbing.

The wide trail becomes a narrow stony path, and runs by a huge glacial erratic (deposited by the receding glacier 15,000 years ago) shaped like a beanbag chair.

Watch for ivy. While while a nuisance to humans, it nourishes birds who feed on the seeds, which appear in autumn.

3. At the four-way intersection, continue to go straight, following the Blue Trail.

Each summer month you can pick fruit on this trail. In July, blueberry bushes offer their small, sweet berries; in August large juicy blackberries are tempting, as well as the sweet, black, crunchy huckleberries; come September **wild grape vines** produce tangy black grapes.

4. At the intersection with the Red Trail, bear left, remaining on the Blue Trail.

5. When you reach a fork in the trail, bear left to climb to the top of Peaked Hill.

A large boulder marks the lookout. Looking south, you'll see a vista of the sandy shoreline bordered by ponds of assorted sizes. Out in the ocean lies Noman's Land, a small government-owned island. If you glance out to the west, you'll have a great view of Aquinnah and its lighthouse. To the north, on a clear day you may be able to pick out all four Elizabeth Islands: The island to the left is Cuttyhunk which contains the town of Gosnold, the governmental center of the islands. A narrow channel separates Cuttyhunk from Nashawena. The third island is Pasque and the largest, to the left, is Naushon.

6. Retrace your steps down Peaked Hill and turn left onto the Yellow Trail on your way to Radar Hill.

The trail passes a cow pasture protected by an electrified fence. This pasture had been part of the subdivision. The financially distressed developer stripped the fertile topsoil and sold it. The farmer who is leasing the land, together with the Lank Bank, have worked together to reconstitute the soil.

| Black-eyed Susan | Hay-scented fern | Wild grape vine |

Judging from the variety of wildflowers, the soil reclamation has been successful.

7. At the next intersection, turn right, remaining on the Yellow Trail, which follows the pasture. Keep your eye out for cows grazing nearby. The birdhouses on the farmland were placed there to attract **American kestrels**, also known as **sparrow hawks**: small, very fast hawks with rust-red colored backs and tails and double black stripes on their white faces. If the hawk is in flight, look for long, pointed bluish-gray wings and listen for its shrill "killy, killy, killy."

To view another panorama ascend the steep path to the Radar Hill lookout marked by radar equipment on the top.

At the beginning of WWII, the military acquired one acre of this elevated eastern location and installed a radar station and access road here. During the Korean War, the government added a communications facility. The property became conservation land in 1970 when the government auctioned it off to residents, who donated the land to the Vineyard Open Land Foundation. The foundation transferred the property to the town of Chilmark.

8. Cut across the wide circular universal access trail to the sign that points to "Peaked Hill Trail Network."

9. Continue to cut across the wide trail to a narrow trail.

10. Cross the road, remaining on the Yellow Trail.

11. Bear right at the fork with a blueberry bush in its center to return to the parking area.

TRIP 16
WASKOSIM'S ROCK RESERVATION

Location: Chilmark
Rating: Moderate
Distance: 4 miles
Food and Drink: Cronig's Up-island Market on State Road in West
    Tisbury.

**Equally enjoyable for hiking or off-road biking, Waskosim's
Rock Reservation boasts the largest acreage (185) of any
single property owned by the Martha's Vineyard Land Bank.**

Directions
The reservation is located off the left side of North Road 1.5 miles west of
the junction with State Road, and just after the Chilmark town line sign.

Trip Description
Waskosim's Rock Reservation offers well-maintained trails that wind
through varied terrain filled with a mix of wildflowers, birds, and trees.
The reservation is named after an immense boulder that dominates one of
the highest hills on the Vineyard. A huge crack running down the middle
of Waskosim's Rock has inspired numerous local legends and created many
photo opportunities.

The Route

1. From the parking lot, head onto the Blue Trail.

2. At the first intersection, turn left, remaining on the Blue Trail.
    The boardwalk of hand-hewn cedar planks crosses a wetland that con-
tains many species of moisture-loving plants. The **sweet pepperbush,** with
its spiky white flowers which perfume the summer air, and the **swamp azalea,** whose white blooms give off a cinnamon-like odor, are two of the more
pleasant-smelling plants. One that doesn't smell as pleasant is found growing low to the ground next to the boardwalk. If you sniff **skunk cabbage**
where its large leaves connect to the fleshy stem, you'll know how it got its

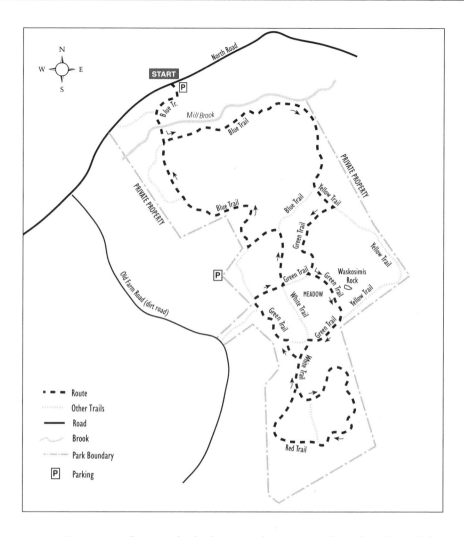

name. **Cinnamon ferns**, which thrive in damp areas, line the sides of the trail. At the end of the bridge, a grove of **wild sarsaparilla** grows beside the path. Look for an umbrella-shaped leaf with three layers. In summer, clusters of greenish-white flowers hide below the leaves.

Wooden steps to protect old stone walls lead to a trail interspersed with tree roots, rocks and hunks of granite. On your left, the Mill Brook parallels the path.

This moss-covered trail meanders back and forth over the brook amid groves of maple and beech trees. **American holly** trees and **sassafras** trees, with mitten-shaped leaves, also grow alongside the trail.

3. At a junction marked by a Land Bank sign board, turn left onto the Yellow Trail.

The trail runs by a stone wall and cuts through a meadow crisscrossed by many stone walls. The walls are remnants from the days when stones lying in the fields were piled on top of each other to contain cows and sheep that grazed the land. The foundation sitting in the meadow belonged to the Allen family, who farmed the land more than 100 years ago.

Birdfeeders scattered across the meadow draw a variety of birds, including bluebirds, doves, bobwhites, starlings, robins, swallows, goldfinches, crows, and hawks in search of prey.

Keep your eyes open for **box turtles**, which are the size of tortoises and have an orange and brown pyramid pattern on their shells. **Sumac bushes** and **chokecherry** saplings dominate the field, but interspersed you may see, in late summer or fall, fuzzy white clusters of small flowers named **hyssop-leaved thoroughwort**, which is also known as **boneset.** The name "boneset" came from herb doctors who used the plant to heal broken bones. **Queen Anne's lace** blooms all summer, displaying flat-topped clusters of tiny white flowers. Its leaves resemble those of its ancestor, the carrot. Like the carrot, its long taproot can be cooked and eaten.

4. At the next fork bear right and then continue straight onto the Green Trail. Be alert to green Land Bank markers attached to trees. The path leaves the meadow and heads into the woods passing a huge glacial erratic in the shape of a skullcap.

The small lacy, delicate fern growing in the shady areas is called **maidenhair fern**.

In summer, juicy, black huckleberries, growing on both sides of the trail, provide an energy boost for hiking the upcoming hills.

5. After the second short incline, bear right at the fork onto the Green Trail.

6. Now at the top, continue straight on the Green Trail.

Swamp azalea

Holly

Maidenhair fern

Further up the trail, on your right, may be a view (in early spring and late fall when there is no foliage on the trees) of the Vineyard Sound foothills, including the adjacent Mill Brook and surrounding valley. This deep narrow valley was known for generations as Zephaniah's Holler, named after Captain Zephaniah Mayhew, one of the early settlers on Martha's Vineyard.

7. Keep bearing left at all intersections until you reach Waskosim's Rock, the immense boulder on your left.

8. Continue past the rock and bear right, remaining on the Green Trail.

9. Turn left at the fork, onto the White Trail.

10. Turn left, remaining on the White Connector Trail.

11. Turn left onto the Red Trail. This narrow trail climbs and then descends amid an understory of ferns, huckleberry bushes and poison ivy.

12. After completing the loop, turn right and retrace your steps on the White Trail.

Waskosim's Rock

Waskosim's Rock and all the smaller boulders that surround it were deposited by a receding glacier. The rock's original silhouette was altered by a bolt of lightning that created a fissure down the center, large enough to conceal two or three people. Rumor has it that Waskosim's Rock was once a favorite hideaway for fugitives.

The American Indian Chiefs Nashawakemmuck and Takemmy probably gave the rock its name when they began the tradition of having the boulder serve as a boundary between their properties. Matthew Mayhew, a Vineyard settler, continued this tradition by using the rock to separate his land from those belonging to the Wampanoag. This boundary, called the Middle Line, was defined by a stone wall that ran from the rock straight to Menemsha Pond. The land to the north of the line belonged to the Wampanoag and to the south, Mayhew.

A 6-foot square, flat-topped boulder near the base of the rock makes a perfect picnic table. Many years ago, when the Vineyard consisted mainly of farmland and was not so densely forested, Waskosim's Rock could be seen from a great distance and was a popular visiting place. Farmers brought their families to the site to picnic and enjoy the view.

Oak branches seeking sun on the Blue Trail.

13. Take the next left and hike up the Green Trail.

14. Bear right at the fork, remaining on the Green Trail as it continues to ascend.

When you reach the top of the hill, climb the large boulder for a bird's-eye view of the meadow.

15. Bear right, staying on the Green Trail as it travels on the opposite side of the meadow that you hiked earlier.

In the early morning and late afternoon during spring and fall, this spot is popular with bird-watchers.

16. Take the next left onto the Blue Trail.

17. Turn right following the blue blazes and the North Road Trailhead sign.

18. Continue straight across the stone bridge to return to the parking lot.

TRIP 17
GREAT ROCK BIGHT PRESERVE

Location: Chilmark

Rating: Generally easy walking but the descent to the beach is fairly steep.

Distance: 1.5 miles, including beach walk; 0.4 mile is a universal access loop; 0.5 mile direct route to the beach.

Restrooms: Located on the left of the trailhead.

Food and Drink: The Galley, the Deli, and Menemsha Market are located in Menemsha, 2 miles southwest of the preserve.

Take this short hike to a secluded beach and hop in the water for a swim.

Directions

The preserve is located on the right side of North Road, 3.7 miles west of the intersection of State, North and South Roads in West Tisbury, 1.2 miles west of Tea Lane and just past the Chilmark Fire Station. To reach the parking lot and trailhead, proceed 0.5 mile down the entrance road and look for the white Land Bank sign.

A bike rack is located in front of the caretaker's cabin.

Trip Description

Finally—a spot on the north shore where you can hike and swim! Great Rock Bight Preserve, a recent acquisition by the Martha's Vineyard Land Bank, was worth the wait. It offers a universal access, shady, wide, level walking trail with benches where you can stop to admire vistas of Vineyard Sound and the Elizabeth Islands. A steeper trail leads to a sheltered bay where the "great rock" guards a sandy beach that runs for 1,300 feet beside the calm waters of Vineyard Sound.

Bring beach shoes if you plan to swim, as the coast may be rocky. Get there early as there are only eighteen spaces in the parking lot.

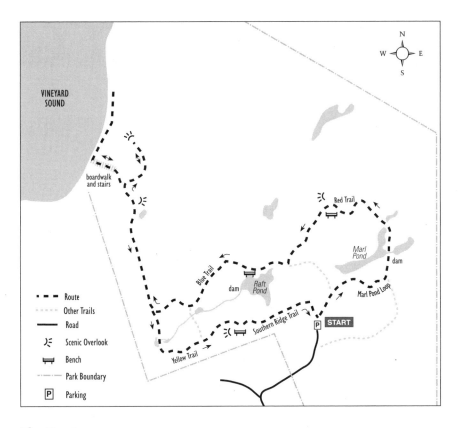

The Route

One of the earliest owners of this property was Elisha Amos, a Wampanoag who died in 1763. He married his slave, Rebecca, who inherited his land and continued to farm here until she died in 1801.

This area not only was used for farming but also provided materials for a brick factory. In the mid-1800s, workers dug clay, formed bricks and baked 600,000 of them a year. Trees were chopped down to fuel the ovens that baked the bricks. After twenty years of operation, all the trees on the land had been felled. With no fuel, the factory closed and the property reverted to farmland.

1. From the trailhead, walk down the path and turn right to begin the Marl Pond Loop.

A boardwalk crosses over Marl Pond, an artificial pond excavated by the former owners to provide water for their livestock. This shady moist area attracts several varieties of ferns. The aptly named **marsh fern**, growing to the left of the first boardwalk, thrives in damp soil. Look for a delicate fern whose leaves grow opposite each other on a smooth, pale green stalk.

Sassafras trees also prefer moist areas and are common to these woods. Their unusual combination of three-lobed, two-lobed, and single-lobed leaves make them easy to spot. Under the trees grows **Indian cucumber root**. Early American Indian inhabitants were fond of the root, which smells and tastes a lot like cucumber. To identify Indian cucumber root, look for a plant with two layers—one whorl of oblong leaves above, and another below. Its small yellow-green flowers emerge from the top layer in spring. At the same time of year the **starflower** produces two small, white, star-like flowers that pop out from the center of five or six shiny dark-green leaves.

In late summer many of the hundred varieties of asters dot the woodland. The **small white aster** is typical of asters that seek these moist open places.

2. At the junction with the Blue Trail, turn right to head down toward the beach.

Raft Pond, also artificial, appears on the left. You may spot snapping and painted turtles resting on the banks. If the Land Bank staff has trimmed the tree tops, the bench may offer a terrific view across Vineyard Sound to the Elizabeth Islands.

3. Turn right, remaining on the Blue Trail, to begin your descent to the beach.

4. Bear right at the fork for a quick stop at the lookout for a spectacular panorama that encompasses Aquinnah on the left and the Elizabeth Islands ahead (the largest, Naushon, is straight on).

5. Return to the trail and turn right toward the beach

Here you'll find ferns that grow in dry areas, such as the delicate, medium-sized, yellowish-green **New York fern**. To distinguish the New

Indian cucumber root   *Starflower*   *White aster*

The great rock submerged in the bight.

York fern from other varieties, look for three or more leaves rising from its root stock.

Sun-loving plants that grow in this arid environment include beach pea, beach rose and seaside goldenrod. In spring, **beach pea** decorates the sand with dainty purple flowers that turn to pods in summer. The bright yellow flowers of **seaside goldenrod** and **asters** contrast with the **beach rose's** pink blooms.

In the lower, moister sections, **sweet pepper bush** with its sweet-smelling, lacey white blooms, line the trail.

Proceed down the steps to the beach where you will discover how this preserve got its name. In the water stands the "Great Rock," in the middle of the "Bight," which is defined as "a wide bay created by a curve in the shoreline."

6. If you wish, you can explore the bight.

7. To return, head back on the same trail.

8. At the fork, bear right onto the yellow-blazed Southern Ridge Trail to return on the second half of the loop.

This open area is filled with grape vines and blackberry bushes. After walking about five minutes, you'll come to a cluster of **tupelos**, also called black gum. On Martha's Vineyard they are referred to as beetlebung trees. In autumn, their small, shiny, green oval leaves turn bright red.

9. Turn right to return to the parking lot.

TRIP 18
MENEMSHA HILLS RESERVATION

Location: Chilmark

Rating: Moderate: Wear shoes suitable for hiking up hills and descending slippery gravel. Take along a water bottle, as many trails are exposed so you may dehydrate quickly on a sunny day.

Distance: 3.5 miles

Restrooms: A portable toilet hides behind a lattice cedar fence at the rear of the parking lot.

Food and drink: At the end of North Road in Menemsha Village, the Galley specializes in lobster rolls and soft-serve ice cream. Next door, the Menemsha Store sells a variety of food and drink.

Hike varied topography and see outstanding views as you explore this 211-acre reservation.

Directions

The reservation is located on the north side of North Road, 1 mile east of Menemsha Village and 4.7 miles west of the intersection with State Road in North Tisbury.

Trip Description

The reservation boasts four different ecosystems, including a mile of rocky coastline. The high point of a tour of Menemsha Hills is hiking to the top of Prospect Hill to view a panorama of both the north and south coasts.

The Route

1. From the parking lot and bike rack, head north toward the trail map board. Pick up the trail behind the board.

2. Bear left at the fork to begin the Harris Loop, marked with red blazes.

In July the trail is brightened by clusters of small white flowers that grow on tall **maple-leaf viburnum** bushes. Surrounding the viburnum are numerous blueberry bushes that reward the hungry hiker with juicy berries.

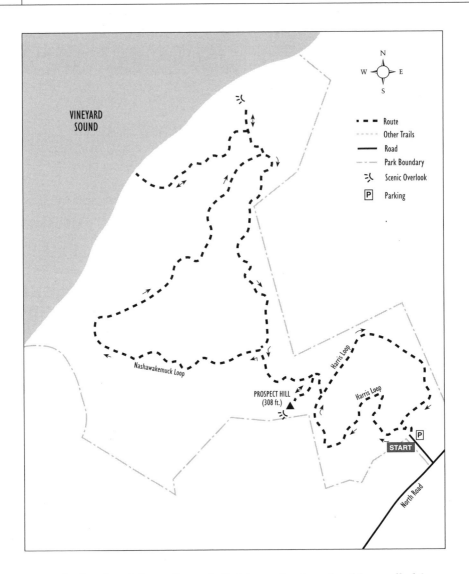

On both sides of the trail stand glacial erratics, large boulders pulled from bedrock by the ice sheet as it inched its way southward. When the ice melted, the boulders remained.

3. At the fork, bear left.

4. Turn left again to continue your climb to the peak.

The pile of rocks on the boulder is a competitive effort to add a few feet to Prospect Hill, so at 313 feet it will be 2 feet higher than Peaked Hill and thus win the distinction of being the highest point on the Vineyard.

Prospect Hill marks the furthest reach of the last glacier that moved southward from the Hudson Bay area about 15,000 years ago. During its slow journey, the glacier collected much of the surface landscape; when it melted, it deposited its accumulation of stones, boulders, clay and other debris. This glacial deposit, called a terminal moraine, formed Prospect Hill. Further evidence of glacial melt is seen along the rocky beach.

From the peak, looking north at the water you can see Vineyard Sound, the Elizabeth Islands, Buzzards Bay and the Massachusetts coast. If the day is clear, you may spot all four Elizabeth Islands: Cuttyhunk, Nashawena, Pasque, and Naushon. A western view includes Menemsha and its harbor, Lobsterville Beach, and Aquinnah with its lighthouse. To the southwest, you'll see Menemsha Pond, Squibnocket Pond and the Atlantic Ocean.

5. Retrace your steps and turn left onto the trail that leads to the Nasha-wakemuck Loop. The path passes under an old, wide, multi-stemmed scrub oak. Hopefully, it won't fall victim to the same fate as the dead oaks nearby, which did not survive several summers of assault by caterpillars.

The path crosses a dirt road and then weaves through an area whose topography is quite different from Prospect Hill. In August and September, the attractive but poisonous red mushrooms, **Emetic russula**, dot the woods.

Watch your footing on your descent, as you savor views of Vineyard Sound, Aquinnah, and Lobsterville Beach.

As you descend further, you enter a forest of spindly-stemmed **horse chestnut** trees. Look for pinwheel-shaped leaves with five, six or seven leaflets. In late spring, the horse chestnut tree displays white, bell-shaped flowers. In late summer, it produces a brown spiny capsule that contains two poisonous chestnut-like seeds. Horse chestnut trees prefer moist soil and usually grow in or near wetlands.

Grapevines flank the path before it crosses a small wooden bridge that traverses the lowest point of the reservation.

6. After hiking approximately 1 mile on this lower trail, turn left, following the yellow blazes toward the beach.

A short side trail on the right leads to a lookout boasting a panorama, with exceptional views of the Elizabeth Islands. Woods Hole and Falmouth are part of the large land mass on the far right. On a clear day you can see the Gay Head Lighthouse off to the left.

A near view on the right reveals a chimney poking through the trees and a boulder perched in the water. The chimney belonged to a brickyard that occupied the land a century ago, and the boulder is the namesake "Great Rock" of Great Rock Bight Preserve, described in Trip 17.

7. Return to the path and continue on the trail down to the beach.

Bearberry, the ground-hugging plant with tiny, shiny green leaves, covers the ledge on both sides of the trail. On your descent into a sunny valley with a great vista of Vineyard Sound and the Elizabeth Islands, you'll see a variety of colorful wildflowers decorating the plain. The white flower with lacy leaves is called **yarrow**. ***Rosa rugosa's*** pink blossoms cover the hillside. Stay away from the poison ivy encroaching on the trail.

Jump down onto the rocky beach. The glacier deposited rocks and boulders on the northern side of Martha's Vineyard. Because the southern side is made up of outwash—sand and gravel that flowed from the melting glacier—the beaches there are sandier and usually rock-free.

8. To return, retrace your steps on the same trail.

9. After passing the overlook, turn left to complete the Nashawakemuck Loop.

This section is shorter and less steep. It is filled with unusual oak trees which have several trunks and long branches that extend out rather than up. These multiple trunks may be due to sheep having grazed on the oaks' new shoots or farmers repeatedly cutting down the trees. These determined saplings then sent out more shoots and grew additional stems. Their branches grew horizontally for two reasons: an adaptation for protection from continual wind blasts and to ensure that each branch received as much sun as possible.

10. At the fork, following the red blazes, bear left to return to the Harris Loop. Recross the road, cut through a stone wall, and pass the path to the top of Prospect Hill.

Red maple

Horse chestnut tree

Yarrow

North shore views from the reservation overlook.

11. Turn left to complete the Harris Loop.

The trail descends through a moist wooded section covered with ferns. Among the varieties is the **northern lady fern**. Look for a lacy fern that grows in a circular cluster. Do not get too attached to the prickly greenbrier vines and blackberry bushes.

It's much easier to identify the **tupelo** trees on the left side of the trail in autumn, when their small green leaves turn bright red. Tupelos are also known as black gum but on the Vineyard they're referred to as beetlebung trees. This name is derived from the "bungs" or plugs for whale oil barrels that were made from the trees' dense wood. "Beetle" is the name given to the hammer used to pound in the bungs.

12. Turn left to return to the parking lot.

TRIP 19
GAY HEAD CLIFFS AND BEACH

Location: Aquinnah

Rating: Easy: Short climbs from the beach to the parking lot and to the top of the cliffs; level beach walking.

Distance: A short climb to the top of the cliffs; a ten-minute walk down to the beach, and unlimited beach walking.

Restrooms: There is a fee to use the bathrooms adjacent to the parking lot. Free portable toilets sit next to the boardwalk at the beach entrance.

Food and Drink: Several fast-food shops line the cliffs. For sit-down dining and great views, head for the Aquinnah Restaurant on top of the cliffs.

Fees: The Gay Head Lighthouse, open only in summer for 1½ hours before sunset and 1 hour after sunset, charges adults $5.00. Children under 12 may enter for free.

View the majestic Gay Head Cliffs from above and below.

Directions
Travel west on South Road to your first stop in the town of Aquinnah. Continue 1 mile to reach the beach parking lot. The beach is located south of and below the parking lot. The viewing area at the top of the cliffs sits north of and above the lot.

Trip Description
Choose a clear sunny day to fully appreciate the panorama from the top of Gay Head Cliffs and for strolling along the beach. From the sand, your eyes will be drawn first to the majestic cliffs, rising steeply to flaunt their colorful striations and then to the beach-goers, in bathing and birthday suits, prancing in and out of the water and often wallowing—illegally—in the clay pits.

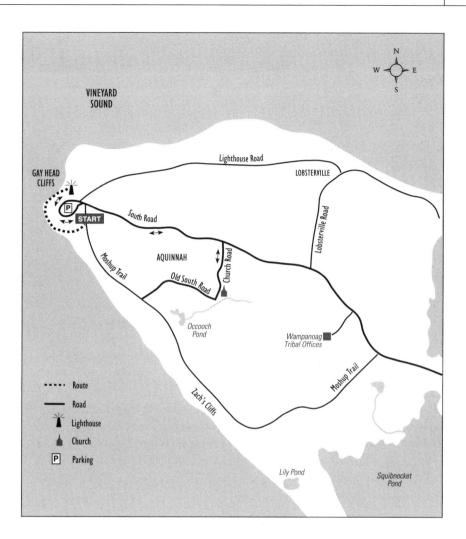

The Route

1. Aquinnah Center is comprised of a volunteer firehouse, the town hall containing the police station, and across the street, a library housed in a former one-room schoolhouse.

The schoolhouse was built in 1827 and enlarged in 1857. Boys and girls entered separately through its two doors.

2. Turn left onto Church Road, to the left of the library. This street becomes Old South Road and continues to Moshup's Trail.

Boulders, beach, and Gay Head Cliffs. Although Gay Head changed its name to Aquinnah in 1998, the cliffs and lighthouse continue to be identified with the town's former name.

Bear left onto a gravel road to see the **Community Baptist Church,** the oldest American Indian Protestant church in continuous existence in North America. This little white church, with its nine rows of pews and pressed tin ceiling, first welcomed Wampanoags in 1859. The original nineteenth-century lamps light the small chapel; only now instead of using kerosene, the lamps use electricity.

One explanation why the Wampanoag community on Aquinnah has survived for hundreds of years is that there was no overlap between the church and tribal culture. Each was always kept separate so the church did not replace the native culture nor did the native culture change to fit Christian doctrines.

3. Proceed 1 mile to the beach and cliffs parking area.

4. From the parking lot, head up the steps to the viewing area at the top of the Gay Head Cliffs.

Although Aquinnah is now the least populated Vineyard town, its location at the tip of the island was preferred by American Indians because it allowed them to easily travel north, south, or west. The Aquinnahs were proficient sailors and thus were in demand for guiding whaling ships through these treacherous waters. When colonists arrived on the island, the Aquinnahs shared their knowledge of the sea and also taught them how to cook fish and shellfish on the sand—the predecessor of our seaside clambakes.

Look directly north for a splendid seascape of the Elizabeth Islands. The island furthest to the left is Cuttyhunk, the governmental center of the chain. Cuttyhunk appears larger than it actually is because the angle of vision conceals the water that separates it from Nashawena, the island to its right. The next island is Pasque, followed by Naushon. The land mass beyond the islands is Cape Cod.

The **Gay Head Lighthouse**, perched on the cliffs directly to the right of the viewing area, warns ships away from the wide reef that extends a mile into the water. The original lighthouse was built in 1799. Its exterior and inner workings were made of wood that expanded in damp weather, forcing the lighthouse keeper and his wife to turn the light by hand. The current lighthouse, now made of brick, replaced the wooden one in 1844. Twelve years later, it was outfitted with a Fresnel lens that captivated the World's Fair in Paris, where the lens won a gold medal. Now the lens rests in the Vineyard Museum in Edgartown, where it is maintained by the Martha's Vineyard Historical Society.

Glimpse below the lighthouse for an excellent view of the striated cliffs that end in a secluded beach.

The Gay Head Cliffs were created during the Ice Age. Glacial movement and melting forced the upheaval of deposits formed millions of years ago. These deposits, flattened into layers, or striations, colored with shades of red, green, brown and gray, contain sediments formed during a specific geological period consisting of thousands and often millions of years. Some layers are composed of fossils, shells, or ancient vegetation, while others consist only of sand or gravel. This upheaval, combined with thousands of years of erosion, has enabled geologists to detect in the cliffs' various shadings and textures the remnants of life, as it was, during the past hundred million years.

5. To head to the beach, return to the parking lot.

6. Find the boardwalk at the southern side of the parking lot and follow it to the beach.

7. Now at the beach, turn right.

This hike is as good as beach walking gets. Because the beach follows the cliffs around the western tip of the island, the vista out into the ocean continually changes. The cliffs, the only constant, loom over the beach, providing a multi-colored presence at your side. Their colors vary depending on your location, the weather and time of day: from mid-day tones of amber and slate to warm reds and oranges at sunset. As the ocean encroaches, these exposed layers of sedimentary deposits are being worn away.

The beach's southern side displays an assortment of rocks scattered by the frequent storms that have battered this shore. The beach tends to be sandier on this side and families settle here to swim and picnic. Once you round the bend and head up the rockier northern coast, you'll notice changes in both the beach and its occupants. Because this section is more remote, it attracts couples who wish to sun and swim unencumbered by bathing suits. Some wallow in the clay at the foot of the cliffs and emerge coated with the dirt. However, environmentalists are rightfully concerned about the clay bathing, since it accelerates the already rapid erosion of the cliffs. Now the clay baths are illegal and anyone caught partaking of that pleasure pays a hefty fine.

Once you reach the tip, look out into the ocean for the small, uninhabited **Noman's Land Island**. This island was not always deserted. In the nineteenth century, Vineyard fishermen spent at least six months a year there, lobstering in summer and fishing for cod in spring and fall. However, now Noman's Land Island is living up to its name and is used only by the United States Navy for bombing practice.

If you continue to walk the beach, you will reach the secluded section that you observed from the top of the cliffs.

8. Whenever you finish your tour, do an "about face!" and return.

TRIP 20
GAY HEAD MORAINE

Location: Aquinnah
Rating: Easy
Distance: 0.8 mile
Restrooms: Located below the shops at the cliffs and at the entrance to the beach on Moshup's Trail.
Food and Drink: A variety of fast food shops at the cliffs 2 miles west.

This short hike can be combined with a trip to the Gay Head Cliffs and/or the beach.

Directions
From the intersection of State and Lobsterville Roads, go north on Lobsterville Road 0.5 mile. Go right on the dirt road for 0.1 mile. There are two parking areas: one for the Universal Access trail and one for the Woodland Loop trail.

Trip Description
Three different environments (meadow, woodland and wetland) provide plenty of variety on this short hike through a section of this 90-acre preserve. A shorter universal access trail leads to a viewing platform that offers a panorama of Menemsha, the north coast and Vineyard Sound. Because of the wetlands, bring mosquito repellent.

The Route

1. Walk behind the Land Bank information board and head for the sign to "Views and Trail Loop."

The name of this property, "Moraine," indicates that this section of the island marks the furthest reach of the last glacier that moved southward from the Hudson Bay area around 15,000 years ago. During its slow journey, the glacier collected much of the surface landscape; when it melted, it deposited its accumulation of stones, boulders, clay and other debris in this area.

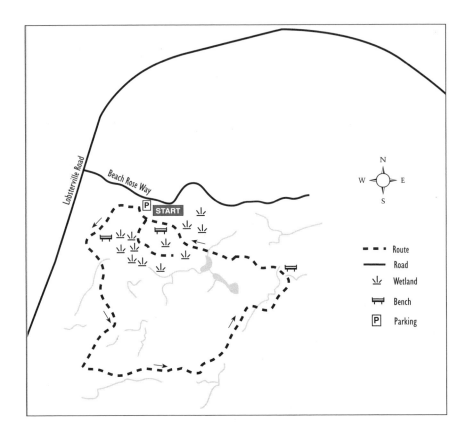

Following your climb up the short incline, you can rest on the wood plank bench and admire the views of Menemsha Village and the north shore.

A variety of wildflowers grow in the meadow. When I was there one August I saw chicory's bright blue blooms. **Chicory** not only is pleasing to the eye, it also was used as a love potion. Several hundred years ago a gentleman would drop its seeds in the drink of his favorite female in the hope that she would be more attentive to him. Chicory also has been used as a mild sedative, for skin irritations, and to prevent scurvy. It originally was brought from Europe so that settlers could continue to roast and grind its fat root for use as a coffee substitute. Now it is added to coffee beans to enhance their flavor.

Also growing in August were small round white flowers of the **hyssop-leaved thoroughwort**, originally used to help heal broken bones, which explains its other name, "boneset."

Now leaving the meadow, you will notice different varieties of plants that indicate a wetland environment. **Sweet pepperbush**, which thrives in

| Chicory | Hyssop-leaved thoroughwort | Sensitive fern |

moist places, is a medium-sized shrub that produces clusters of small white, sweet-smelling flowers. **Sassafras** trees, one of my personal favorites, also prefer damp conditions. You've probably heard of sassafras because its bark and roots are used to make tea. Sassafras is the only tree I know that boasts three different shaped leaves, one mitten-shaped, one three-lobed and the third with a single lobe.

The trail loops into a woodland. A bench is positioned to overlook a brook running through a ravine.

2. From the bench, bear left at the fork and cross a boardwalk positioned over the brook.

Lacey **lady ferns**, which grow in circular clusters and thrive in moist, semi-shaded conditions, grow on each side of the boardwalk.

As the path descends, you'll see another variety of tree that thrives in a damp environment. The **horse chestnut** grows seven leaflets that form a circle. Other moisture-loving plants that grow beside the path are **sensitive ferns**, whose broad triangular leaves make them look most un-fernlike and **cinnamon ferns**, very large ferns that grows in circular clusters.

The path passes under a canopy of horse chestnut saplings and then climbs over a stone wall protected by wooden stairs.

Once you ascend from wetland to woodland, you'll see many rudimentary stone walls, an indication that this area once had been a farm. Grapevines and greenbrier vines dominate the woodland. The **rattlesnake fern** enlivens the landscape with its bright green color.

The end of the trail is marked by several wooden plank bridges.

The universal access trail goes by the gazebo (which was already on the property when the Land Bank purchased it) and to the viewing platform.

2

On-Road Biking on Martha's Vineyard

Martha's Vineyard has a great reputation as a biker-friendly destination for good reasons. Although the island is only 23 miles long, it boasts 37 miles of bike paths, which are perfect for families. An added advantage is the island-wide system of bike-rack-equipped buses, which have bailed out many tired cyclists.

Choosing a Destination

The rides in this book vary in length and difficulty in order to appeal to a wide range of ages and abilities. Don't let the distances intimidate you. Since most roads are flat, it's easy to cover 15 to 20 miles in two hours. You'll have many opportunities to catch your breath during the frequent stops that are built into the trips. Do allow enough time for your explorations so you can leisurely investigate whatever is of interest.

Each of the on-road biking trips originates from one of the three most populous towns: Edgartown, Vineyard Haven, or Oak Bluffs. I have included directions from the other two towns so cyclists can pedal the route from any of the three starting points. Most of the bike rides form loops so you can explore different terrain on your return. These trips contain maps with detailed explanations of the routes, interesting sights along the way, and locations of conservation areas and public restrooms, along with shops where you can buy food and drink.

The directions are numbered to help guide you. Each successive number indicates a change in direction. If faced with a situation where there is no number or directional change, continue straight. Additional information—

Bicycles locked up near the beach.

historical, botanical, and geological—is indented below the direction. This format gives you the choice of reading this information or skipping over it to focus only on the directions.

Although all the trips ride mostly on paved surfaces, six will take you on short off-road portions. Your bicycle model will make some destinations more or less accessible. Unless you own or can rent a mountain or hybrid bike, you will find riding on unpaved roads quite challenging. A mountain or hybrid bike will give you greater traction on the sometimes-sandy bike paths, better maneuverability on dirt roads, and the option of biking off-road. If you have a touring bike and are determined to reach a specific destination, you may have to walk your bike on these sandy or rocky sections.

Safety and Etiquette

Even though Martha's Vineyard is a terrific place for cyclists and the bike paths will protect you from most road hazards, there are risks to watch for:

1. Driveways and side roads that intersect the bike path. Drivers do not always notice cyclists on bike paths. Always slow down and check to see if a vehicle is approaching; if one is, **assume that it will not give you the right of way**. Make eye contact with the driver before passing in front of his or her vehicle.

2. Pedestrians. Joggers and walkers also use bike paths. Pedestrians usually yield if you say "excuse me," followed by "on your left" or "on your right," depending on which side you will be passing. When passing, be sure to look ahead for traffic coming from the opposite direction.

3. Other cyclists. Many riders ride two or three abreast on the path. Others stop in the middle. Again, a polite "excuse me," followed by your passing direction should suffice.

4. Sand and gravel. Sand is everywhere on the island. Watch out for skidding when turning or braking.

While on bike paths, follow the rules of the road. Ride single file on the right hand side. If you have to stop, pull over to one side so you will not obstruct traffic. If possible, try to pass on the left.

Not every Vineyard road has a bike path, so you often will have to share the road with cars, trucks, motorcycles, and mopeds. Although the routing in this book protects you from riding on the busiest and most dangerous roads, you will encounter traffic, particularly during July and August. Your best protection is to be alert, defensive, and cautious. Hug the side of the road. Use hand signals. Ride single file. Wear a helmet.

Before setting out on your exploration, make sure you have the necessary gear. Also check your bike carefully to prevent being stranded because of faulty brakes or a flat tire. Hopefully, you will not need the emergency phone numbers and addresses listed in the appendix at the end of this book.

Rating: Easy: bike paths run along 12 miles of the route.

Distance: 16.4 miles

Food and Drink: Vineyard Haven, near the Steamship Authority Terminal: Black Dog Bakery, Stop& Shop Supermarket, Mad Martha's; in the Tisbury Market Place on Beach Road: Net Result; Oak Bluffs, across from the Steamship Authority Terminal: Lookout Tavern.

Restrooms: Vineyard Haven: at the rear of the Steamship Authority Terminal; Oak Bluffs: in the Steamship Authority Terminal on Beach Road.

This tour of the three largest towns on Martha's Vineyard is interspersed with spectacular seascapes.

Trip Description

Eye-popping panoramas just keep on coming—from Lagoon Pond in Vineyard Haven to the headwall overlooking Nantucket Sound at East Chop in Oak Bluffs, and along the barrier beach beside Sengekontacket Pond! Swimming is possible anywhere along the 2-mile-long Joseph A. Sylvia State Beach.

The Route

Edgartown bikers: Pick up the directions at No. 8.

Oak Bluffs bikers: Pick up the directions at No. 7.

1. Begin at the Steamship Authority Dock at the end of Union Street in Vineyard Haven. Because of heavy traffic, I suggest walking your bike to Water Street and then turning left.

2. Continue walking your bike past the Black Dog Bakery on the left and the Stop & Shop across the street. Both stores can supply you with food and drink to take on the trip. At the busy "Five Corners" intersection, bear left onto Beach Road, heading toward Oak Bluffs.

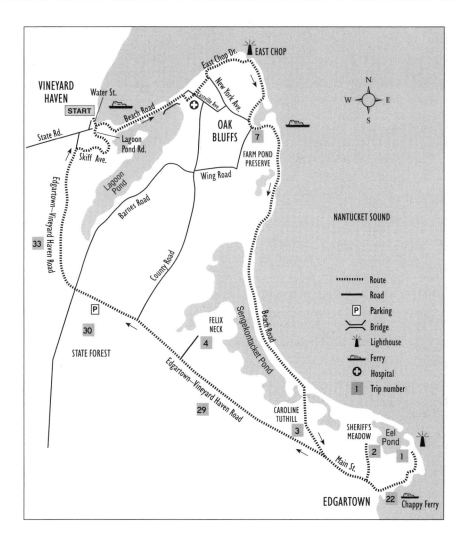

3. A narrow bike lane offers some protection from the traffic.

On the right, The Net Result, one of the shops in the Tisbury Market Place, sells fresh and cooked fin and shellfish that you can take home or eat outside on the picnic tables.

Soon after, on the right, sits Winds Up, a water sports store, where you can take kayaking and windsurfing lessons on Lagoon Pond.

Just past Winds Up, a bike path begins and extends for 0.3 mile to the public boat landing.

Beach Road becomes a causeway, crossing Vineyard Haven Harbor on the left and Lagoon Pond on the right. The Vietnam Veterans Memorial Bridge at the end of the causeway marks the boundary between the towns of Vineyard Haven and Oak Bluffs. If your timing is right, you won't have to wait for the drawbridge to open so boats can travel between the pond and the harbor. When a hurricane or nor'easter is forecast, boats line up in the harbor to pass under the bridge so that they can wait out the storm in Lagoon Pond. The bridge is in the process of being replaced and a temporary one is being built next to the original bridge. I have been told that there will be bike lanes on both the new and temporary bridges.

4. Soon after crossing the bridge, watch for the Bike Path signs. Turn right onto the short path that protects you from a dangerous stretch of road.

5. The bike path ends across from East Chop Drive. Dismount and carefully cross the road to pedal on **East Chop**.

On Martha's Vineyard, there are two "Chops"—East and West. Here "chop" refers to an opening to a body of water. Both chops rise high above Vineyard Sound, protecting the entrances to Vineyard Haven and Oak Bluffs Harbors.

As you bike along East Chop Drive, look on your right at **Crystal Lake**, formerly known as Ice House Pond. Before the advent of refrigeration residents used ice from this pond to keep their food from spoiling.

Proceed to the **East Chop Lighthouse**, perched high on the bluff, where you can dismount and enjoy the panorama. To the left lies Vineyard Haven Harbor and West Chop. Falmouth, a town on the southern edge of Cape Cod, is the land mass directly ahead.

Continue your loop around the bluff. For a panoramic view of Edgartown, Chappaquiddick, and then Cape Poge, stop just after you pass Atlantic Avenue on the right. This bluff provides an excellent vantage point for observing the activity below. Ferries from Hyannis, Falmouth, and Woods Hole continually shuttle passengers back and forth. Although small, the Oak Bluffs Harbor claims never to turn a boat away, so there is a constant stream of pleasure craft motoring in and out.

As you proceed around the Chop, just before the opening to the harbor, on the left you'll see the East Chop Beach Club, a swimming, sailing, and tennis complex for families who summer on East Chop.

6. At the T intersection with Lake Avenue, turn left. Follow Lake, past the Oak Bluffs Harbor. If you wish to visit the **Camp Meeting Grounds** (Trip 7), proceed from this point.

7. Continue straight, heading toward the ocean and ferry terminal. When Lake Avenue becomes a one-way street, turn right onto Seaview Avenue (The Steamship Authority terminal will be on your left).

As you leave Oak Bluffs Center, you'll pass two parks: the first, **Ocean Park,** hosts summer band concerts and the annual fireworks display. After passing the second, Waban Park, you'll come to **Farm Pond**, home to two metal sea serpents. **Farm Pond Preserve**, a twenty-seven acre property owned by the Martha's Vineyard Land Bank, occupies the land in front of the pond. A trail winds through marsh grass to the water.

Harthaven, a small community located on the south side of Farm Pond, is named after its settlers, the Harts. Look on your left for Harthaven's miniscule harbor.

The bike path begins in 0.6 mile as the name of the road changes to Beach Road. Since you travel straight on this road until you reach Edgartown, you don't have to worry about missing a turn. However, be wary of other cyclists. Because this route is flat and winds by spectacular shoreline, it is the most popular path on the island. Not everyone knows the rules of the road, so keep right and remain alert.

On your right is the **Farm Neck Golf Course**. Because of the panoramic water views from many of its holes, Farm Neck is regarded as the most scenic course on the island.

Just ahead is the beginning of the **Joseph A. Sylvia State Beach**. Early morning swimmers frequent this beach for their daily exercise. Windsurfers, too, favor this beach because of its calm seas and steady winds. In midafternoon, when the wind picks up, the more adventurous windsurfers jump on their boards.

Less adventurous windsurfers attempt the sport on the other side of the road in the less intimidating Sengekontacket Pond. If the tide is low, windsurfers may be joined by clammers, since the pond supports an abundance of shellfish. In autumn, Sengekontacket is a popular scalloping spot.

If you decide to swim, you can park your cycle in a bike rack in a small parking lot on the left side of the road at the southeast end of the beach.

During late spring and early summer a common island shrub, ***Rosa rugosa*** flaunts its delicate pink blossoms. This sun-loving plant thrives in sandy soil so it is commonly found alongside roads and beaches. In fall its blossoms become shiny red round hips which are a great source of vitamin C.

A group of bikers riding alongside Nantucket Sound.

The beach ends at a little stream named Manada Creek. Late in the day, young and old, armed with nets, wade in the creek and search for blue-claw crabs.

8. After cycling 5 miles from the Steamship Authority Terminal, you will reach the intersection of Beach Road and the Edgartown-Vineyard Haven Road. This intersection forms a wedge called the Great Harbor Triangle, which hosts a variety of shops and a few restaurants. To reach the **Edgartown** (Trip 1) and **Sheriff's Meadow Sanctuary** (Trip 2) walks and the **Chappaquiddick** (Trip 22) bike ride, continue straight onto what is now called Upper Main Street. Cannonball Park is wedged between the convergence of Upper Main Street, Cooke Street and the Edgartown-West Tisbury Road.

9. To continue the loop and/or to visit the Caroline Tuthill Wildlife Preserve or Felix Neck Wildlife Sanctuary, turn right at the bicycle sign into the Great Harbor Triangle parking lot.

10. Proceed through the lot, cross the Edgartown-Vineyard Haven Road and turn right onto the bike path.

The obscured entrance to the **Caroline Tuthill Wildlife Preserve** (Trip 3) is located on the right side of the Edgartown-Vineyard Haven Road, 0.5 mile from the Beach Road intersection. Within the preserve, which sits on the shore of Sengekontacket Pond, is a 1.3-mile loop through 154 acres of woodlands.

One and a half miles farther, on the right, lies the Felix Neck Wildlife Sanctuary (Trip 4), a 350-acre preserve owned and operated by the Massachusetts Audubon Society. More than a hundred species of birds have been observed in and around this sanctuary.

Less than a mile from the entrance to Felix Neck is a development known as **Dodger's Hole**, which is named after a glacial kettle hole that can be seen through the clearing on the left about 300 feet beyond Dodger's Hole Road.

This glacial kettle hole was formed about 15,000 years ago when the glacier that covered Martha's Vineyard began to melt and recede. A large block of ice separated from the glacier and became buried in the earth, leaving a very large hole when it melted. Because this deep hole lay below the water table, it formed a pond. However, Dodger's Hole is rapidly drying up and is now more bog than pond.

One mile from Dodger's Hole Road is Martha's Vineyard Regional High School. Sanderson Avenue, the access road to the Manuel F. Correllus State Forest, lies between the school building and the playing fields. The starting point for the State Forest to Thimble Farm off-road ride (Trip 30) is 1 mile down Sanderson Avenue.

Just ahead, at the intersection with Barnes Road, is the "blinker," the only traffic light on the island. Of course, there are other intersections that could use a traffic light, but Vineyarders balk at any mechanized reminder of the mainland.

11. After the bike path ends, cross the Edgartown-Vineyard Haven Road and pedal toward Vineyard Haven. Continue 0.4 mile and take the third right onto Skiff Avenue. This maneuver not only escapes the traffic heading into Vineyard Haven but also allows a great downhill run.

12. Turn left at the T intersection onto Lagoon Pond Road.

13. Carefully cross at the perilous "Five Corners" intersection to Water Street. Follow Water Street to the Steamship Authority Terminal.

TRIP 22
CHAPPAQUIDDICK RIDE

Rating: Easy: flat terrain. The last mile is unpaved and sandy.

Distance: 12.8 miles round-trip from Cannonball Park.

Fees: Chappy Ferry: $6.00 round-trip for cyclists. Wasque
Reservation: $3.00 per person.

Food and Drink: Edgartown: Village Market and Rotisserie, 199 Main
Street, next to the Mobil Station and across from the western tip
of Cannonball Park; Soigné, gourmet take-out, 190 Main Street, at
the junction of Cooke and Main. Chappaquiddick: Chappy General
Store, located on the left side, 2.2 miles from the ferry landing.
You can refill your water bottle at the hand pump at Wasque
Reservation or at the water fountain at Mytoi.

Restrooms: Edgartown: On the left side of the Visitors' Center
on Church Street between Main Street and Pease's Point Way.
Chappaquiddick: At Mytoi, East Beach and Wasque Reservation.

**With its small size, flat terrain, little traffic, and lack of rout-
ing hassles, Chappaquiddick is perfect for biking.**

Directions

To get to Chappaquiddick, take the Chappy Ferry that runs continually between Edgartown and Chappaquiddick.

Trip Description

Since there is only one paved road on Chappaquiddick, it's almost impossible
to get lost. "Chappy" also offers mellow off-road cycling so you can alternate
pavement with pine-needle-covered paths.

You will discover there is not much happening on the island. Its residents
enjoy the outdoor life and prefer the absence of commercial activity. During
the ride, you can stop to swim at Chappy Point Beach, East Beach, and/or
Waque Reservation, rent kayaks at East Beach and paddle around Poucha
Pond, as well as explore four conservation areas on bike or foot.

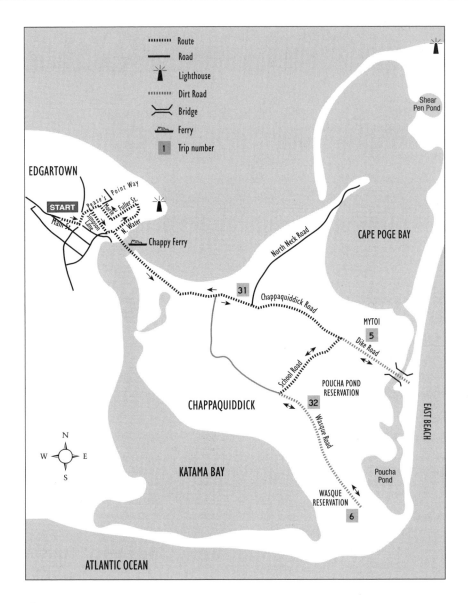

The Route

1. From Cannonball Park (also known as Memorial Park), the wedge of land formed by the junction of Upper Main Street, Cooke Street, and the Edgartown-West Tisbury Road, proceed east on Main Street toward Edgartown Center.

2. Pedal two blocks and turn left onto Pease's Point Way, following the Bike Route signs.

3. Turn right, remaining on Pease's Point Way, following the signs to the Chappy Ferry.

4. Proceed two blocks past the bike parking area on Pease's Point Way until you reach Simpson Lane. (The road on the left side is named Pierce Lane!) Turn right, following the Bike Route and Chappy Ferry signs.

5. Proceed two blocks to North Water Street. Turn left.

6. Immediately turn right onto Daggett Street. The Chappy Ferry signs are clearly posted at this turn.

7. Ride down the short stretch to the ferry landing. The cars parked to your right are waiting to drive onto the ferry; however, bikers do not have to wait. Park your bike to the right of the loading platform where there may be an attendant to collect fees ($6.00 round-trip for cyclists; no money is collected on the return trip). Wait until cars, bikers and pedestrians disembark. After the two-minute ferry ride, the attendant will indicate when to get off.

The Wampanoag and European Settlers

Chappaquiddick was inhabited by the Wampanoag Tribe for nearly 10,000 years before colonists arrived. These American Indians used simple tools to work the land and subsisted on such foods as corn and shellfish. In cold weather they lived inland, and when the weather grew warmer, they moved closer to the ocean.

The English arrived in 1642, and soon began to use the land on Chappaquiddick for grazing sheep and cattle. In October of each year, the farmers drove their livestock to the middle of the island, where the animals would spend the winter. Come spring, the sheep were herded to a pond in Cape Poge Bay where they were washed and shorn of their wool. This pond continues to bear the name Shear Pen Pond, reflecting how it was used three hundred years ago.

Settlers did not reside on Chappaquiddick until the middle of the eighteenth century, when Edgartown became a major whaling port. At that time, a lighthouse was erected on Cape Poge to guide ships into busy Edgartown harbor, and ship captains and their crews began to move to Chappaquiddick. By 1778, 42 settlers and roughly 1,000 Wampanoag lived on the island. By the end of the nineteenth century vacationers began to summer here.

An island of beetlebung tupelo trees in the middle of Brine's Pond.

Before 1920, the cost to cross the channel was only a few cents; however the only way over was in a rowboat and one had to ring a bell to call the ferryman. Large items were hauled across the water in a barge.

Chappy Point Beach, to the left of the ferry slip, offers a great view of Edgartown Harbor. Here you can watch the parade of boats motoring in and out of Katama Bay, with stately Edgartown residences in the background.

8. Proceed 1.3 miles from the ferry. North Neck Road on the left is the starting point for the **Three Ponds Reservation** off-road bike ride (Trip 31).

The Chappy General Store, which carries a little of everything, is located on the left side, 0.7 mile from North Neck Road.

9. A half-mile past the Chappy General Store, the paved road swings sharply right. To reach **Mytoi** and **East Beach** (Trip 5), continue straight onto the dirt road. Mytoi lies 0.5 mile down the road. Dike Bridge and East Beach is 0.2 mile further.

Because of Chappy's limited access, most people were not aware of its physical attributes until 1969 when Senator Edward Kennedy drove his car off Dike Bridge. The highly publicized death of passenger Mary Jo Kopechne drew droves of people searching for "The Bridge." Some of these visitors discovered that Dike Bridge leads to East Beach, a glorious 5-mile-long barrier beach. Chappaquiddick's new notoriety, combined with the 1970s building boom, created a demand for homes that produced the first surge of population growth in one hundred years. Even today, many people continue to associate this little island with Dike Bridge and the Kennedy tragedy rather than with its other considerable physical attributes.

To continue the ride toward Wasque, remain on the paved road for 0.8 mile until you reach the junction with Wasque Road.

10. Turn left onto Wasque Road. Continue 0.8 mile to **Poucha Pond Reservation** (Trip 32). You can explore the reservation on bike or foot.

Soon after Poucha Pond Reservation, a mile-long stretch of stony, rutted, sandy road begins. To best navigate this road, shift into a low gear so your bike wheels will spin and give better traction. Keep your wheels straight to keep your bike from skidding on the sand. When you encounter soft, sandy sections, you may have to dismount and walk your bike until the surface becomes firmer.

If you decide to explore **Wasque Reservation** (Trip 6), you will receive a monetary award for negotiating this challenging road: you won't have to pay the $3.00 automobile entrance fee, but during the summer season you will have to pay $3.00 per person to swim, hike, and bike.

11. To return, proceed down Wasque Road. Turn right onto School Road.

12. At the junction with Chappaquiddick Road, bear left for the 2.5-mile ride back to the On-Time Ferry, so named because two ferries cross the short distance between Chappaquiddick and Edgartown in minutes, ensuring that one of the ferries is always at each shore.

13. After disembarking from the ferry, you must walk your bike up Daggett Street (one-way) to North Water Street. Turn right.

The houses on the left side of North Water Street were built at an angle so their occupants—families of captains of whaling ships—would have a better view of the boats sailing into the harbor. After you pass Morse Street, look up onto the roof of the second house on the left. The balustrade on the top, called a "widow's walk," enabled captains' wives to look far out into the ocean as they anxiously awaited their husbands' return.

Just before the road bends, look to your right at the **Edgartown Lighthouse**. The original lighthouse was built in 1828 on a small artificial island a quarter-mile out into the harbor. One could access it only by boat; however, the next year a footbridge was built. In 1938 the structure was replaced, but, by then, it no longer sat on an island, since ocean currents had created a sandbar between the lighthouse and the mainland. A mile-long public beach extends from the lighthouse to Eel Pond.

14. Continue around the bend and turn left on Fuller Street. Colorful gardens decorate the side yards of these attractive old homes.

15. Fuller ends at Morse Street. Turn right.

16. Take your second left onto Pease's Point Way.

17. Follow Pease's Point Way as it bends around and intersects Main Street. Turn right.

18. Remain on Main Street back to Cannonball Park.

TRIP 23
SOUTH BEACH AND KATAMA POINT LOOP

Rating: Easy; much of the trip is on bike paths
Distance: 23.3 miles round-trip from the ferry terminal in Vineyard Haven.
Restrooms: Vineyard Haven: In the Steamship Authority Terminal on Union Street. Edgartown: Next to the bathhouse at the Katama entrance to South Beach.
Food and Drink: Vineyard Haven: Union Street, Black Dog Bakery, Stop & Shop, Mad Martha's; on the Edgartown-Vineyard Haven Road, Norton Farm; Edgartown: Upper Main Street, Stop & Shop, Dairy Queen and The Fresh Pasta Shoppe; on the corner of the Edgartown-West Tisbury Road and Meshacket Road, Morning Glory Farm.

This panoramic beach ride—perfect for a sunny, balmy day— takes you along a 2-mile stretch of sandy beach pounded by crashing waves.

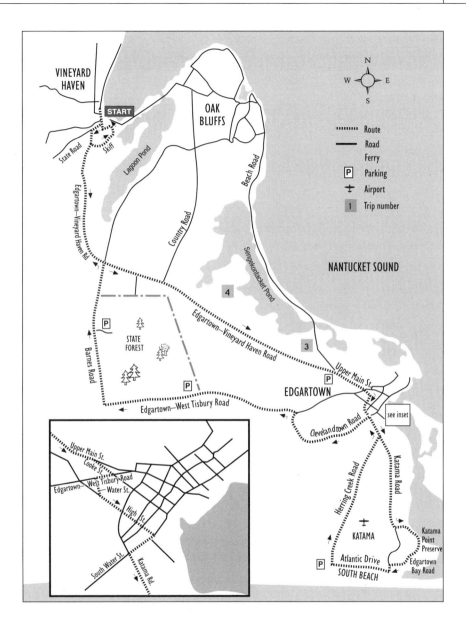

Trip Description

A trip to Katama Point and South Beach, located at the southeastern tip of Martha's Vineyard, offers a great ride, much of it on bike paths, as well as a cool, scenic destination. An added advantage to going by bike is that you won't have to search for a place to park at one of the most popular beaches on Martha's Vineyard. And there is even a bathhouse for changing.

The Route

Oak Bluffs Bikers: Follow the directions in the West Tisbury South Loop (Trip 25) to the intersection of County Road and the Edgartown-Vineyard Haven Road. Turn left toward Edgartown and pick up the directions at No. 6.
Edgartown Bikers: Begin the following directions at No. 8.

1. From the Steamship Authority Dock on Union Street, take the first left onto Water Street.

The Stop & Shop Supermarket and Black Dog Bakery are conveniently located for stocking up for the trip. You also will pass many other restaurants and stores on the Edgartown-Vineyard Haven Road in Edgartown.

2. Hook a right through the Stop & Shop Parking Lot which leads to Main Street. (This maneuver is called COCC—"Cutting Off Crowded Corners.")

3. Turn left on Main Street. You will have to walk your bike since Main is a one-way street.

4. Main ends at State Road. Turn right and continue walking your bike up this short, steep, congested stretch.

5. Turn left on the Edgartown-Vineyard Haven Road toward Edgartown. The bike path begins in 0.6 mile and continues for 6.6 miles.

If you want to purchase fresh produce, Norton Farm is 1.4 miles up the road. The Martha's Vineyard Community Services complex is located 1.2 miles east of Norton Farm. The buildings house such services as early child-hood programs, a counseling center, substance abuse help, and emergency psychiatric service.

The wooded area across from Community Services and behind the Martha's Vineyard Regional High School is the 4,343-acre Manuel F. Correllus State Forest, half of which lies in Edgartown, the other half in West Tisbury.

Two miles from the high school on the left side is **Felix Neck Wildlife Sanctuary** (Trip 4), a great place for youngsters to walk trails, and to view exhibits and wildlife.

Another area with easy walking trails is the **Caroline Tuthill Wildlife Preserve** (Trip 3) located on the left, 1.5 miles past Felix Neck.

6. The Edgartown-Vineyard Haven Road intersects with Beach Road, form-ing a wedge of land named the Great Harbor Triangle, filled with shops and restaurants. After the intersection of these two roads, the street name changes to Upper Main Street. Continue on Upper Main, past the commercial establishments.

7. At the fork bear right onto the bike path on Cooke Street, following the signs to Katama and South Beach. On the left side of Cooke Street sits **Cannonball Park,** the departure point for explorations that begin in Edgartown.

8. Take the first right onto the Edgartown-West Tisbury Road. Cross the road to access the bike path.

9. Take your first left onto Roberts Way, just before the brick school. Follow this road past the cemetery to the intersection with Pease's Point Way.

10. Continue through the next intersection onto High Street, following the Katama Beach Bike Route signs.

11. Follow High Street for three blocks to the T intersection with S. Water Street. Turn right.

This scenic but convoluted bypass is Edgartown's attempt to remove bicyclists from a narrow, dangerous section of road.

12. Remain on S. Water to the first intersection, Katama Road. Turn left and proceed to the bike path on the left side of the road.

The farmland on the right is used by the Farm Institute as a teaching farm. Its mission is to educate and engage children and adults in sustainable agriculture through the diverse operations of a working farm.

13. Proceed on the bike path on Katama Road for 2 miles to Edgartown Bay Road. Turn left.

14. This road loops, paralleling Katama Bay. Proceed on this road, bearing left at the fork, for 0.7 mile.

Just before the road begins to loop around, look on your left for the partially hidden Land Bank logo sign and Katama Point Preserve. If you reach the town landing parking lot, you have gone too far and should retreat 750 feet.

Katama Point Preserve, a two-acre parcel of land owned by the Land Bank Commission, juts out into Katama Bay and offers an extended view of Edgartown and its harbor, as well as the southern end of Chappaquiddick. Here, bird-watchers enjoy spotting shorebirds, such as cormorants, least terns, and the osprey family nesting on a pole in the center of the property.

You can swim here in the calm waters of Katama Bay or wait until you reach South Beach where you can jump in the waves and body surf.

If you wish to visit the preserve, park your bike in the bike rack and head down the trail toward the water. You'll spot the osprey pole on the left. There has been a recent resurgence in ospreys due to the installation of these poles. The island osprey population had diminished due to a lack of dead trees, the natural nesting sites of ospreys, which are fish-eating hawks. Volunteers, working in conjunction with the telephone company, installed telephone poles all over the island to provide safe nesting sites. As you explore the island, you'll notice other nesting poles.

Continue on to the beach. Because Katama Point protrudes out into Katama Bay, you can see miles of Edgartown coastline, including its harbor (the bay is explored by kayak in Trip 34). Directly ahead lies Chappaquiddick, now an island due to the mile-long breach in the barrier beach that was the connector to South Beach. Only eleven times in the last two hundred years have violent storms created openings in this barrier beach. The openings can take as long as ten years to fill.

Picnicking, fishing, and swimming are permitted here, but if you prefer a larger sandy beach and surf, return on the same trail to pick up your bike and continue on to South Beach.

15. At Edgartown Bay Road, turn left toward the entrance to South Beach.

Bike racks line the road near the intersection with Atlantic Drive. North of the road lies Mattakeesett Herring Creek, an artificial ditch that connects Katama Bay to Edgartown Great Pond.

The original Herring Creek was created in 1728 and drew 700,000 herring that swam here annually to spawn. This second Herring Creek was excavated at the end of the nineteenth century to replace the first creek. Because of beach erosion, this creek now lies about a mile out in the ocean. Early Vineyard maps show a series of fresh water ponds also swallowed up by the sea. Rumor has it that Vineyarders used to ice skate from Katama Bay to Edgartown Great Pond on these interconnected ponds.

If you wish to visit South Beach, park your bike and walk onto the beach. Over the last 20 years, I have noticed a marked diminution in the width of the beach. The reason: the ocean is encroaching on the south coast at an annual rate of 8 feet a year. As you walk, you'll notice some sections of beach have been totally swept away, leaving only sand dunes.

If you are seeking solitude, head east toward Chappaquiddick. The farther you walk, the fewer people you'll see. Four-wheel drive vehicles can reach these remote sections by driving in through the motorists' entrance, located to the left of the main entrance. Drivers must buy a permit and be able to navigate a narrow sandy strip that extends 1.5 miles to the beach.

Vehicles are not allowed on the beach when baby piping plovers and least terns are in residence.

This eastern section of beach parallels Katama Bay; you can either walk by the surf or along the edge of the bay. If you cross from the ocean side to the bay, avoid walking on the fragile sand dunes. Dunes help to slow beach erosion; the higher they are, the less the ocean can encroach on the land.

Least terns, which look like a skinny seagull, often nest in this section. In order to increase the diminishing tern population, conservationists have roped off the tern nesting areas.

In this remote section, you'll be more likely to spot **sandpipers**, tiny birds with long bills, who appear to be racing back and forth on the sand chasing each receding wave. What they really are doing is searching for sand fleas that emerge from little openings in the wet sand to feed on plankton carried in by the surf.

If you want to swim, head back to the mile-long lifeguard-supervised section of the beach. If the waves are high, there often will be a strong undertow.

Riptides, strong currents that flow rapidly away from shore, occasionally have trapped unsuspecting swimmers. Lifeguards advise swimmers caught in the rip to swim at a right angle to the flow, parallel to the shore, until out of the current.

16. When you are ready to leave the beach, retrieve your bike and turn left onto Atlantic Drive.

17. Atlantic Drive runs for 1 mile to Herring Creek Road, the second entrance road to South Beach. Turn right. The bike path is now on the left side of the street.

On the right you will pass Katama Air Park, a grassy landing field for small private planes and gliders.

Ahead on the right is the 28-acre Waller Farm, purchased jointly by the town of Edgartown and the Land Bank Commission in order to preserve island farmland.

18. At the intersection with Katama Road turn left.

19. Take your first major left onto Clevelandtown Road. This road curves around for 1.8 miles, and changes its name in the middle to Meshacket Road. It passes the now-closed Edgartown dump and then Morning Glory Farm, located on the corner of the Edgartown-West Tisbury Road, which sells fresh produce and baked goods.

20. Turn left onto the bike path on the Edgartown-West Tisbury Road.

21. Continue on the path for 1.4 miles when the path crosses from the south to the north side of the road. The path continues for another 1.7 miles to Barnes Road.

22. Turn right onto Barnes Road. The bike path is on the left side of this road and is hidden from view.

23. Pedal for 2 miles to the 4-way stop signs and "blinker," the only traffic light on Martha's Vineyard. Turn left on the Edgartown-Vineyard Haven Road toward Vineyard Haven.

24. After the bike path ends, cross to the right side of the road, proceed 0.4 mile and take your third right onto Skiff Avenue.

25. Enjoy the downhill, enhanced by a view of Lagoon Pond. Turn left, at the end of the descent, onto Lagoon Pond Road.

26. Lagoon Pond Road joins four other roads at the hazardous "Five Corners" intersection. Walk your bike across the road and then continue on Water Street.

27. At Union Street, you can either turn right toward the ferry dock or left toward Mad Martha's and reward yourself with an ice cream cone.

TRIP 24
VINEYARD HAVEN, WEST CHOP, AND HERRING CREEK BEACH

Rating: Easy: Flat terrain with little traffic, 6.7 miles of bike paths
on the paved roads, very sandy on the last stretch of unpaved
road to Herring Creek Beach.

Distance: 17 miles round trip (20.5 with the side trip to Herring
Creek Beach) from the ferry terminal in Oak Bluffs.

Food and Drink: Oak Bluffs: across from the Steamship Authority
on Seaview Avenue, Lookout Tavern; Vineyard Haven: Beach
Road, Artcliffe Diner, Net Result in the Tisbury Market Place,
Union Street, Black Dog Bakery.

Restrooms: Oak Bluffs: in the Steamship Authority Terminal
on Seaview Ave; Vineyard Haven: in the Steamship Authority
Terminal on Union Street and next to the parking lot in Wilfrid's
Pond Preserve

This historic and scenic ride includes sweeping views of Vineyard Sound, Cape Cod, and the Elizabeth Islands.

Trip Description
This trip explores Vineyard Haven, the busiest port on Martha's Vineyard, and then follows the coastline north to West Chop. The grand finale consists of stops at two beaches: Wilfrid's Pond Preserve, a secluded beach which looks onto Vineyard Sound, and Herring Creek Beach, a picturesque peninsula where you can wade in the calm waters of Lake Tashmoo or walk across the sand to swim in the ocean. Since automobile parking is limited for both spots, the beaches are perfect for cyclists who don't mind pedaling over a mile-long unpaved and often sandy road.

The Route
Edgartown bikers: Follow the Edgartown-Vineyard Haven Road to the intersection with State Road in Vineyard Haven. Turn right and then left on Main Street. Pick up the directions at No. 11, turning left on Church Street.
Vineyard Haven bikers: From the Steamship Authority Terminal, go straight up Union Street and pick up the directions at No. 9.

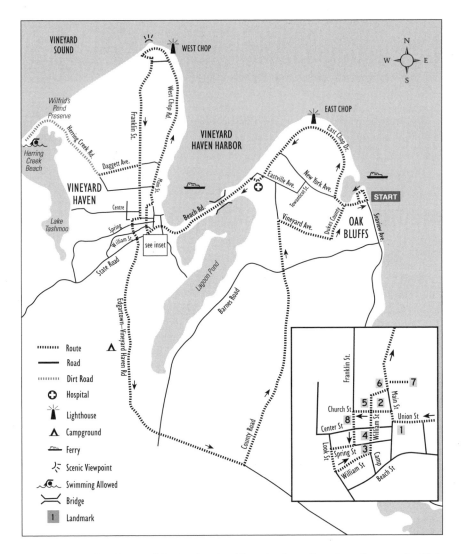

1. Begin at the Steamship Authority Terminal on Seaview Avenue in Oak Bluffs.

2. Turn right on Seaview Avenue and head toward the parking area for cabs, buses, and cars waiting for the Island Queen and Hy-Line Ferries.

3. At the parking lot, turn left and pedal past all the bike and moped rental shops to the main road, New York Avenue.

4. Turn right onto New York Avenue.

From the northernmost tip of West Chop, a view across Vineyard Sound to Cape Cod.

5. Pedal past Oak Bluffs Harbor, and take your first right onto East Chop Drive.

6. Circle around the Chop while enjoying the views of the boats motoring in and out of the harbor.

7. At the end of the Chop, turn right.

8. Cross Eastville Avenue to access the short bike path that replaces a dangerous stretch of road.

9. The path cuts through the grounds of the new hospital and connects to a bike path on Beach Road where you turn left.

Remain on Beach Road for a mile, pedaling on the bike lane on the new drawbridge that spans Lagoon Pond on the left and Vineyard Haven Harbor on the right. Just past the bridge, on the left, lies a boat launching area. Just beyond, a bike path runs for 0.3 mile.

10. At the "Five Corners" intersection in Vineyard Haven, continue straight, passing the Black Dog Bakery on the right, onto Water Street.

Because of the variation in posted signs, visitors can be confused by the two names for this town. Is it Vineyard Haven or Tisbury? Vineyard Haven actually is incorporated into the town of Tisbury, but residents differentiate between the two names by referring to the business district and harbor as Vineyard Haven and the surrounding area as Tisbury.

11. Take your first left and walk your bike up Union Street, which is one-way.

Having reached the middle of the block, look to your left for the **Thomas Chase House** (1 on the map), a simple two-story home. The oldest surviving house in Vineyard Haven, it was built in 1717 by Thomas Chase, a ship captain who was lost at sea in 1721. In order to earn a living, his widow, Jane, turned their well-located home into an inn, named "The Beehive." It remained an inn for 100 years, at which time it became the residence of Admiral Edward Smith of the United States Coast Guard

12. Still walking, turn right on Main Street.

13. Take your first left onto Church Street.

Halfway up the block on the left sits the **Vineyard Playhouse** (2), which provides the island with first-rate theatrical entertainment. It was built in 1835 as a Methodist Meeting House. Twelve years later the Methodists moved across the street into a new church. When it burned down in 1922, it was rebuilt as the stone church you now see across the street. Around 1850, Captain Richard Luce and Charles Smith bought what is now the Vineyard Playhouse for public meetings, added another story and named it Capawock Hall.

The History of Vineyard Haven

Vineyard Haven was settled in 1674, and its original name was Holmes Hole. "Hole" referred to the location of its harbor, protected by the two headlands of East Chop and West Chop. "Holmes" may have been the name of the owner of the adjoining land.

Although Holmes Hole began as a farming community, its protected location on Vineyard Sound destined it to become a popular seaport. By the middle of the nineteenth century, the harbor was second only to the English Channel in the number of ships that stopped on their way to and from Europe, Africa, and the West Indies.

Vineyard Haven thrived, catering to thousands of vessels that harbored in its port. Many residents became pilots and accompanied these ships on their journeys. Others provided sails, navigation equipment, food, and clothing. However, the opening of the Cape Cod Canal in 1914, combined with the increased use of trains, trucks, and steamships to move cargo, reduced the number of vessels passing through Vineyard Sound. Vineyard Haven continues to be the island center for commercial sea traffic, but now its ferries carry passengers who drive the island's main industry—tourism.

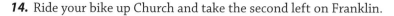

14. Ride your bike up Church and take the second left on Franklin.

15. Ride 2 blocks on Franklin and turn right onto Spring Street.

16. Take your next left on Look Street.

17. Take your next left on William Street.

Across from the intersection with Camp Street at 40 William Street sits the **Captain Richard C. Luce House** (3), a beautifully restored home.

It was built in 1833 for Luce, one of the Vineyard's most successful whaling captains, who paid for the house by first selling whale oil in Rio de Janeiro, where he purchased coffee beans, which he then sold in New England. This Greek Revival-style home was the first of its size to be built in Vineyard Haven. Soon other whaling captains followed Luce's lead and built homes on William Street.

18. Take the first left on Spring Street. Walk your bike (another one-way!) to the third building on the right.

Earlier known as **Association Hall,** and now referred to as **The Tisbury Town Hall** (4), this building was constructed in 1844 and served as a meetinghouse and church for both Baptists and Congregationalists. Now it functions as both the Town Hall and the Katherine Cornell Memorial Theatre. To commemorate Vineyard Haven's 300th anniversary, the actress Katherine Cornell donated funds to restore Association Hall and remodel its theater.

19. Return to William Street and turn left. Pedal past other Greek Revival-style captains' homes.

This street, an officially designated historic district, was spared because the 1883 fire went downhill rather than uphill.

20. After pedaling for 4 blocks (0.2 mile), look on your left for the **Benjamin Cromwell House** (5) *before* you turn right on tiny Colonial Lane (there may not be a street sign). This Gothic revival-style home is quite different from the other Captains' homes because it was built in 1873, 40 years later. Whereas the owners of the other homes were whaling captains or maritime ship masters, Cromwell skippered the old Island Line, a ferry that ran between New Bedford, Martha's Vineyard, and Nantucket. When the Methodist Camp Meetings in Oak Bluffs reached the height of their popularity in 1859, Cromwell's ferry carried as many as 1,500 passengers.

Travel down Colonial Lane to Main Street.

The **Old Schoolhouse Chapel** (6) is situated on the right corner. Its bell tower is what remains of the original schoolhouse, which was built in 1829.

The pole in front of the schoolhouse commemorates three colonial girls who defied British troops during a daring raid. After the school was closed in 1855, the building was first a carpentry shop, then a funeral home and finally a museum. It now is owned by the Martha's Vineyard Preservation Trust.

21. Turn left on Main Street.

22. Take your next right onto Owen Park Road. **Owen Park** (7) contains benches, swings, and a bandstand used during Sunday evening concerts. The park belongs to the town, courtesy of the widow of William Barry Owen, a lawyer who made a fortune by introducing the Victor Talking Machine to Europe. With his newly gained wealth Owen first built a large home on William Street and then tried to buy the homes blocking his view of Vineyard Haven Harbor. He successfully removed three homes that formerly stood on what is now Owen Park.

Continue down the road to the public beach if you wish to swim or sunbathe while watching ferries shuttling in and out of the harbor.

23. Return to Main Street and turn right for the 2-mile ride to West Chop. The road loops around, following the coastline.

West Chop, the Vineyard's northernmost headland, refers to both a geographical location on Martha's Vineyard and a self-contained community with its own beaches, tennis courts, and post office.

West Chop's progression from a sheep pasture to resort community began in 1872. Two sea captains purchased a large tract of land for $400 and then managed to sell the same parcel a few weeks later for $10,000! Fifteen years later, the West Chop Land and Wharf Company turned the area into an exclusive summer resort, transporting its residents from the mainland to the company's new wharf via steamboat. As you bike along the bluff, you'll see grand old gray-shingled cottages, many of which were built during this era.

Just before you reach the tip of the headland, you'll spot the **West Chop Lighthouse**, guardian of busy Vineyard Haven Harbor. The lighthouse was built and moved several times in its history. It began its career in 1817 as a wooden structure, which was rebuilt in brick in 1838. Erosion of the 60-foot bluff required the light house be moved in 1848 and again in 1891.

Proceed until you are at the tip of West Chop (6 total miles). Glance right for a clearing that contains a bench for cyclists to relax and enjoy the splendid panorama. The view from this northern point includes the Elizabeth Islands,

to the left. Woods Hole and Falmouth lie straight ahead. Because the distance between Woods Hole and the Elizabeth Islands is quite small, it often appears as if they are one big land mass. Along with pleasure crafts cruising on this busy waterway, you may spot one of the many ferries traveling between the island and the mainland.

24. Bend left around the point, passing the West Chop Tennis Club. At the fork, bear right onto Franklin Street (there may not be a street sign).

25. Remain on Franklin for 1.3 miles—passing the western edge of West Chop Woods and the entrance to Mink Meadows Golf Course on the right—to Daggett Avenue. It's easy to miss this turn because the street sign is on the left side of the road. Turn right on Daggett to proceed to Herring Creek Beach and Wilfrid's Pond Preserve.

26. Follow Daggett for 0.5 mile to the small Beach sign. Turn right onto Herring Creek Road, a divided road for the first half-mile. (Stay on the left side of the road as it is in much better condition than the right.) Pull off to the side to allow cars the right of way.

27. If you seek a secluded spot to sun and swim, stop at **Wilfrid's Pond Preserve**, 0.8 mile down Herring Creek Road. Watch for the Land Bank sign on the right. Pedal down the dirt road to the small parking area (holds 9 cars). A friendly Land Bank employee is usually at the preserve. To reach the beach, follow the short trail. A side path on the right leads to Wilfrid's Pond.

28. To continue to Herring Creek Beach, remain on Herring Creek Road for 0.4 mile. Some sections are easier to navigate than others. Once you reach the peninsula, the dirt road turns to sand. If shifting into a low gear to spin your wheels doesn't give you enough traction, you may have to walk your bike.

At **Herring Creek Beach** you can choose where to sun and swim. If you turn left, you'll face the shore of Lake Tashmoo. Be careful not to disturb the **least terns** who may be nesting in the sand. Do not attempt to swim in the channel where the water is deep and the current very strong. Do look across the channel to see if the eagle-like **osprey** is perched on a pole, scanning the sea for a tasty tidbit. If it finds one, the osprey will land in the water feet-first to gobble up its prey.

If you turn right, you'll soon be on the lifeguard-supervised stretch of sand adjacent to Vineyard Sound. From this beach, you'll have the same spectacular panorama as at West Chop, including two of the Elizabeth Islands—the largest, Naushon, and tiny Nonamesset. You may also spot Woods Hole and Falmouth on Cape Cod.

29. After leaving Herring Creek Beach, retrace your ride on the dirt road.

30. Turn left on Daggett Avenue.

31. Ride down Daggett to Franklin and turn right.

32. Remain on Franklin for eight blocks until you reach Center Street. The **Association Hill Cemetery** (8), at the corner of Franklin and Center Streets, displays stones that mark the graves of the Vineyard's English settlers. The oldest stone is dated 1770, but most represent the years from 1805 to 1817. To return to Oak Bluffs, continue on Franklin for another block.

33. Turn right onto Spring Street. (Since Spring is one-way, you must walk your bike one block; a worthwhile effort to avoid the congestion on State Road.)

34. Take the first left onto Look Street.

35. Remain on Look for 2 blocks until it ends at State Road. Cross State Road and head up the Edgartown-Vineyard Haven Road toward Edgartown.

36. Proceed on the Edgartown-Vineyard Haven Road for 3.3 miles, passing the "blinker"/4-way-stop intersection. Turn left on County Road.

37. Continue on the bike path on County Road for 2.7 miles. At the four-way intersection with Barnes Road, the bike path crosses to the east side of the road. Turn right onto Vineyard Avenue. The street sign is on a white stake at each side of the road.

38. Follow Vineyard Avenue until it ends at Dukes County Avenue. Turn left.

39. Remain on Dukes County Avenue until it ends at New York Avenue. Turn right.

40. At the 3-way intersection proceed straight to Seaview Avenue.

41. Turn left at Ocean Park to return to the ferry terminal.

TRIP 25
WEST TISBURY SOUTH LOOP

Rating: Easy: Mostly flat with a few short hills.

Distance: 25 miles

Food and Drink: Oak Bluffs: across from the Steamship Authority on Seaview Avenue, Lookout Tavern; West Tisbury: on State Road, Alley's General Store and Back Alley's Café.

Restrooms: Oak Bluffs: inside the Steamship Authority Terminal on Seaview Avenue.

Fees: Long Point Wildlife Refuge

Pedal on bike paths through the center of the island.

Trip Description

Take a trip back in time to when the Vineyard relied more on farming than tourism, by cycling through the agrarian center of the island, West Tisbury. This ride also offers opportunities for off-road biking, hiking, and swimming. Because the loop circumnavigates the forest, much of the pedaling is on bike paths.

The Route

Edgartown cyclists, proceed west 4 miles on the Edgartown-Vineyard Haven Road to the Martha's Vineyard Regional High School. Turn left onto Sanderson Avenue, the road next to the school, and pick up the directions at No. 7.

Vineyard Haven cyclists, follow the Edgartown-Vineyard Haven Road east for 2.7 miles to the Martha's Vineyard Regional High School. Turn right onto Sanderson Avenue and pick up the directions at No. 7.

1. Begin at the Oak Bluffs Steamship Authority Terminal on Beach Road. Head down Oak Bluffs Avenue, the road in front of the terminal, to Lake Avenue. A bike lane is planned for this street, but when it actually will be constructed has not been determined.

2. Bear right on Lake Avenue.

3. Turn left onto Dukes County Avenue, across from Oak Bluffs Harbor. A small pond, Sunset Lake, is on your right. On your left lies the **Camp Meet-**

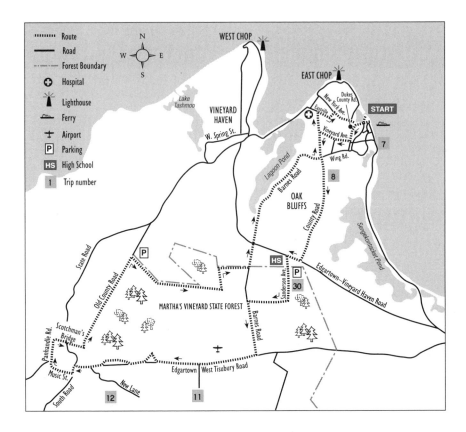

ing Grounds, an enclave of historic Victorian-style homes circling the Tabernacle, described in Trip 7.

4. Take your fourth right onto Vineyard Avenue.

5. Follow Vineyard Avenue to the intersection with County Road. Turn left and access the bike path.

Continue south through the stop-sign intersection with Barnes and Wing Roads as the bike path changes to the right side of the road. A quarter-mile from the intersection, on the left, is a large grass airfield, a portion of the 71-acre **Trade Wind Fields Preserve**, described in Trip 8. You can detour and take an easy 1.3 mile off-road bike ride.

6. Continue on County Road for 2 miles until it ends at the Edgartown-Vineyard Haven Road. Cross the road to access the bike path and turn right (west).

7. The Martha's Vineyard Regional High School is 0.6 mile ahead on the left. Turn left onto Sanderson Avenue, the road that separates the playing field from the school. This road leads to the office of the superintendent of the 4,343-acre **Manuel F. Correllus State Forest** and the starting point for the State Forest, Greenlands, Little Duarte's Pond, and Thimble Farm off-road ride (Trip 30).

8. At the fork, bear right. Do not continue straight toward the State Forest headquarters.

9. The road ends at Airport/Barnes Road. Cross the road to access the dirt trail to the bike path (hidden from view) and turn left.

10. Continue on the bike path for 1.5 miles until you reach the junction with the Edgartown-West Tisbury Road. Remain on the bike path and turn right.

The bike path continues for 3.6 miles, passing the entrance to the airport. An opening on the bike path to the Edgartown-West Tisbury Road (0.3 mile from the entrance to the airport) leads to the entrance road to **Long Point Wildlife Refuge** (Trip 11) on the left. The good news: Long Point boasts a world-class beach. The bad news: You must ride 3 miles down a sandy road to reach it.

The bike path follows, with abrupt ascents and descents, the contour of the glacier-carved land. The path heads into the forest and forms a V, to avoid a wedge of privately owned land.

11. Remain on the path as it passes the back entrance to Hostelling International. Just before the path makes a sharp right turn, a West Tisbury sign marks your left turn toward the Edgartown-West Tisbury Road.

12. Turn right onto the combination bike path/sidewalk toward West Tisbury Center. The bike path ends at the tiny West Tisbury police station.

To explore **Sepiessa Point Reservation** (Trip 12), turn left on New Lane, the first paved road after the fire station.

13. Just after Old Mill Pond, on the right, is the junction with South Road. Bear left toward the center of West Tisbury.

The inviting front porch of Alley's General Store appears on the right. Across the road is the Field Gallery. Sculptor Tom Maley's engaging figures frolic on the lawn.

The **Old Agricultural Hall** sits on the corner of Music Street. On Saturday mornings and Wednesday afternoons during the summer, it hosts farmers and craftspeople who sell their wares.

14. Take the next right onto Music Street. Remain on Music Street for 1.3 miles as the street forms a U.

The farmland on this quiet country road is reminiscent of the island's agrarian past. An additional reminder is the new **Agricultural Society Hall and Grounds,** a mile from the old hall. The new hall and surrounding acreage contain the County Fair, one of the Vineyard's most popular events, which takes place the third week in August. Here, log rolling and oyster shucking contests compete with dog shows, amusement park rides, foodstands, and booths displaying mammoth zucchinis and imaginative flower arrangements.

15. Remain on what is now called Panhandle Road as it crosses South Road. At the next intersection, Old County Road, turn left. Across the road sits one of the island's largest and most popular arthouses, the Granary Gallery.

16. Proceed 1 mile on Old County Road. Turn right, passing through a brown barricade, into the forest to access the bike path.

17. Turn left onto the bike path.

18. Continue on the path for 1 mile. Upon reaching the parking area, turn right onto the 2-mile path that travels east through the forest.

19. At the T intersection, turn left. The path runs north for 0.5 mile and then turns east for another 0.5 mile.

20. Upon reaching another parking area, turn left onto the path that runs beside Barnes Road.

21. Remain on Barnes Road through the intersection with the Edgartown-Vineyard Haven Road. Barnes Road ascends and descends for 2.5 miles, occasionally offering views of Lagoon Pond on the left.

22. Turn left at the intersection with County Road and head onto the bike path on the right side of the road.

23. Remain on County Road to the T intersection with Eastville Avenue. Turn right toward Oak Bluffs.

24. Take your next left onto Towanticut Street.

25. Towanticut ends at New York Avenue. Turn right. Remain on New York Avenue for 1 mile.

26. To escape the traffic on your return to the Steamship Terminal, turn left onto the first side street past the harbor.

27. Continue straight until the road/parking lot ends; turn right onto Seaview Avenue. The terminal is ahead on the left.

TRIP 26
WEST TISBURY NORTH LOOP

Rating: Moderate: A few hills and 1.4 miles of unpaved road, 2 miles of bike paths. Wear brightly colored clothing in order to be easily seen on shaded, narrow, curved roads.

Distance: From Vineyard Haven: 13.4 miles. To include a visit to Cedar Tree Neck Wildlife Sanctuary add 5 miles.

Food and drink: Vineyard Haven, near the ferry terminal: Mad Martha's, Black Dog Bakery; on State Road: Black Dog Café; W. Tisbury: Up-Island Cronig's.

Restrooms: In the Steamship Authority Terminal in Vineyard Haven.

Ride this scenic route to picture-postcard views.

Trip Description

If you seek a rural experience but don't have time for an up-island ride, try this short loop. Rolling country roads, picturesque ponds for cooling off, and several hiking and off-road options contribute to this enjoyable exploration.

The Route

Edgartown Bikers: Take the Edgartown-Vineyard Haven Road to the Steamship Authority Wharf in Vineyard Haven (Nos. 6, 7, and 8 in Trip 21).

Oak Bluffs Bikers: Follow the directions in Trip 24 to Vineyard Haven.

1. Begin at the Martha's Vineyard Steamship Authority Wharf in Vineyard Haven, the main port of entry to the island. Crowds and cars disembarking from the ferry make it necessary to walk your bike straight up Union Street until you reach the intersection with Main Street.

2. Turn right onto Main Street.

3. Take a quick left on Church Street.

4. Now mount your bike and remain on Church for two blocks.

5. Turn left at Franklin Street for one block.

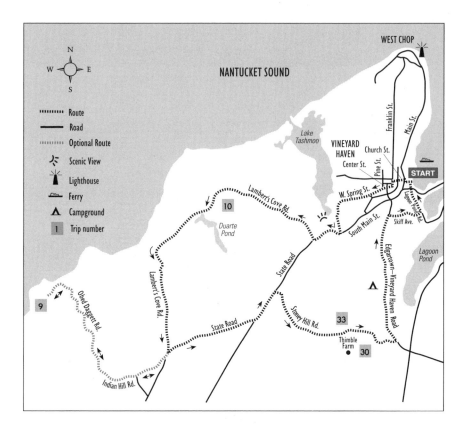

6. Turn right at Center Street.

7. At the T intersection, turn left at Pine Street.

8. Turn right on Spring Street and pass the Tisbury School.

9. At the fork, bear right and remain on West Spring Street for 0.7 mile until the road ends.

10. Turn right onto State Road.

The **Lake Tashmoo Overlook** appears immediately on the right. Pull over to observe a picture-postcard view of Lake Tashmoo and Vineyard Sound beyond. A century ago, a channel was dredged from Vineyard Sound into Lake Tashmoo so that ships could sail into this safe harbor. Before the dredging, the annual dipping for herring in this fresh water pond was a popular springtime activity.

11. Take your next right onto Lambert's Cove Road.

This narrow road twists, turns, ascends and descends for 4.3 miles. Rolling farmland dotted with small ponds and bordered by stonewalls shaded by trees make the effort worthwhile. The road curves around to Lambert's Cove, once a thriving fishing and farming community that had its own ferry running to Woods Hole.

Blackwater Pond Reservation (Trip 10), one of the newer properties owned by the Martha's Vineyard Land Bank, lies 2 miles from State Road and 0.5 mile from the Tisbury-West Tisbury town line sign.

Also on the left, just past the Tisbury-West Tisbury town line sign, lies the remains of the island's last cultivated cranberry bogs. There once were many bogs on the Vineyard, but high transportation costs made it too difficult for the growers to compete with cranberry producers on Cape Cod. The Vineyard Open Land Foundation is seeking funds to restore these bogs.

If you are biking before Memorial Day or after Labor Day, you can visit my favorite beach, Lambert's Cove. (During summer, only West Tisbury residents are allowed on the beach.) The parking lot on the right is 1 mile from Blackwater Pond Reservation and 3 miles from State Road. To see the cove, you must walk a quarter-mile down the path.

Just after the parking lot, also on the right, sits a small quaint white church.

You won't miss **Seth's Pond**, located on the left 0.7 mile from Lambert's Cove Beach. You can see its small sandy beach from the road.

12. Lambert's Cove Road rejoins State Road. If you wish to extend your ride 5 miles on Indian Hill Road and visit **Cedar Tree Neck Wildlife Sanctuary** (Trip 9), turn right on State Road (beware, the mile-long entrance road to the sanctuary is rutted, rocky, sandy, and quite steep).

To extend your ride, take an immediate right onto Indian Hill Road. The long paved driveway on your left leads to Up-Island Cronig's, a food market. Proceed 1.5 miles, until you see a sign on the right for Cedar Tree Neck. Turn right onto the dirt road and follow the sanctuary signs for 1 mile. Don't let all the driveways confuse you. Continue straight on the road until it forks and then bear left. Mountain and hybrid bikes are more suited to this terrain, but all bikers should be wary on this road.

13. To return to Vineyard Haven from Lambert's Cove or Indian Hill Roads, turn left onto State Road.

After riding approximately 1 mile on State Road you have the option of avoiding the traffic and riding 0.7 mile on a newly cut dirt trail. The entrance can be difficult to see as it is on the opposite side of the street and there is only a small wooden sign stating, "Public Walking Path." Start watching for it after you have passed the sign for "Chilmark Potter" and the "40 MPH" speed limit sign. If you reach County Rd, you have missed the entrance but you can still access the path.

14. If on the trail, proceed about 200 feet, or if you have remained on State Road, proceed 1.8 miles from Lambert's Cove Road for 1.8 miles (0.5 mile from County Road), turn right onto unpaved Stoney Hill Road, marked by a wooden shelter for bus passengers. Warning: the road is often sandy and can resemble a washboard.

If you are interested in off-road riding, **Wapatequa Woods Reservation** (Trip 33) is located on the left side, 1.1 miles down Stoney Hill Road.

Across from Wapatequa on a much smoother road lies **Thimble Farm**. In an effort to preserve farmland, the Martha's Vineyard Land Bank purchased the development rights to the farm and has stipulated that the farm can be used only for agriculture. The Land Bank has also cut a trail around the farm (Trip 30).

15. Continue on Stoney Hill Road (the last half-mile is paved, but has many speed bumps) until you reach the Edgartown-Vineyard Haven Road. Turn left onto the bike path toward Vineyard Haven.

16. After 1.4 miles, the bike path ends. Cross to the right side of the road and pedal for 0.4 mile to Skiff Avenue. Turn right on Skiff to escape the congested junction with State Road. It's also a great way to end the ride: a steep downhill, enhanced by views of Lagoon Pond.

17. Turn left at the end of the descent onto Lagoon Pond Road.

18. Lagoon Pond Road joins four other roads at the hazardous "Five Corners" intersection. Walk your bike across the road and continue on Water Street.

19. Water Street meets Union Street. You can either turn right toward the ferry dock or turn left toward Mad Martha's to reward yourself for all those hills you climbed.

TRIP 27
CHILMARK LOOP

Rating: Moderate: Flat terrain until Middle Road in Chilmark, which is hilly; 28 miles of bike paths, plus about 6 miles of cycling on roads in Chilmark.

Distance: Round-trip from Edgartown: 34.5 miles

Food and Drink: Edgartown, on Upper Main Street: The Fresh Pasta Shoppe, Stop & Shop Supermarket; Edgartown-West Tisbury Road: Morning Glory Farm; West Tisbury, on State Road: Up-Island Cronigs; on South Road: Alley's General Store; Menemsha, overlooking Menemsha Basin: Galley Snack Bar, The Deli on Basin Road.

Restrooms: Edgartown, in the Visitors' Center on Church Street, between Main Street and Pease's Point Way; Menemsha, on the east side of the public parking lot for Menemsha Beach and Harbor.

This route offers a great workout, varied landscapes, and many exploratory options, including a picturesque fishing village.

Trip Description

This loop highlights the dramatic physical difference in the island towns: from the rolling farmland of West Tisbury to the Vermont-like landscape of Chilmark. With its antique farmhouses, hilly tree-shaded roads, and rural character, Chilmark more closely resembles northern New England than an island resort community.

You can go for a workout and complete the trip in two to three hours, or opt for a leisurely day trip with possible stops at any of the six conservation areas and the quaint fishing village of Menemsha to swim, stroll, shop, and sightsee.

The Route

For bikers departing from **Vineyard Haven**, follow directions to Aquinnah (Trip 28) to the "blinker" and pick up the directions at No.3.

For bikers departing from **Oak Bluffs**, follow the directions for the West Tisbury South Loop (Trip 25) to the "blinker" and pick up directions at No.3.

1. Begin the trip in Edgartown on the Main Street side of **Cannonball Park**, also known as Memorial Park. This triangular park, landscaped with can-

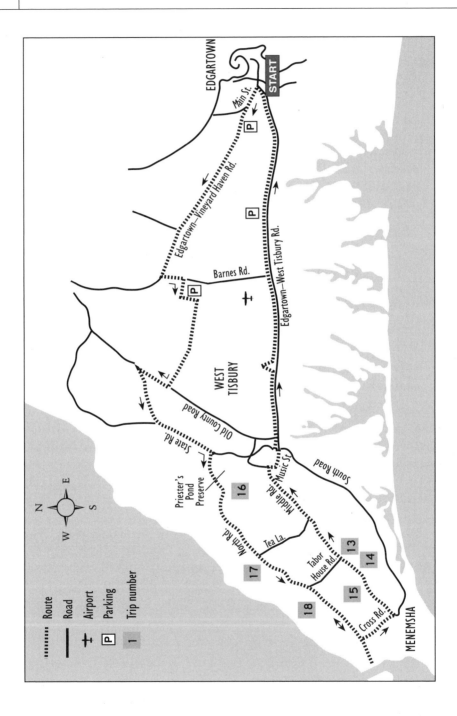

nons and balls from the Charlestown Navy Yard in Boston, memorializes the men who died in the Civil War.

Proceed west on the bike path along Upper Main Street, past a wide variety of stores and restaurants conveniently located for stocking up on supplies before your trip. The Fresh Pasta Shoppe on your left makes sandwiches and pizzas. On your right, the Stop & Shop Supermarket prepares ready-made sandwiches.

2. Continue straight at the fork onto the Edgartown-Vineyard Haven Road. Remain on this road for 4 miles until you reach the 4-way stop sign and "blinker," the only traffic light on the island.

3. Turn left (south) at the blinking red light onto the bike path on Barnes Road.

4. Proceed 0.5 mile down Barnes Road, and turn right onto the bike path that heads into the State Forest. The path travels west for 0.5 mile and turns south for another 0.5 mile.

5. After completing the half-mile south, keep your eyes open for an *easy-to-miss* path emerging from the right. Turn right and bike 2.2 more miles through the forest.

6. Pedal past the barrier to Old County Road. Turn right.

7. After pedaling 1 mile you'll reach State Road. Turn left. Remain on this road for 2.6 miles, following the signs first to Aquinnah and then to Menemsha.

After 1.5 miles you'll see the Up-Island Cronig's Market on the right where you can stop for food or drink.

8. At the junction of State and North Roads, bear right, following the sign toward Menemsha.

On the left corner of the junction lies **Priester's Pond Preserve**, a small but special Land Bank property. Leave your bike in the rack at the North Road entrance and walk down the short path to Priester's Pond. The path forks. A left turn skirts the edge of the pond and crosses a tiny bridge with a waterfall below. A right turn leads to a log bench at the edge of the pond, where you can rest, reflect and rejuvenate.

Up the road 1.5 miles sits the West Tisbury/Chilmark town line sign. Shortly after this sign on the left lies **Waskosim's Rock Reservation** (Trip 16), a great spot for hiking and off-road biking. If you are interested in swimming in a bay with no crowds, continue 2.2 miles to **Great Rock Bight Preserve** (Trip 17), located on the right, 0.5 mile down a dirt road. For hiking,

A view from Middle Road of a farm perched above the Tiasquam River.

continue on to **Menemsha Hills Reservation** (Trip 18), also on the right, one mile west of Great Rock Bight.

9. To complete the Chilmark Loop, turn left in 0.5 mile onto the Menemsha Cross Road; but if you wish to visit the tiny fishing village of Menemsha, continue straight on North Road.

The Wampanoag word **Menemsha** means "place of observation," and, indeed, this picturesque village is a great place to look around. Located in the town of Chilmark, Menemsha is bounded by Menemsha Pond, Menemsha Basin, and Vineyard Sound.

A right turn on Basin Road, the first street on the right after the steep downhill into Menemsha, leads to **Menemsha Beach**. Situated next to the harbor, this small public beach draws throngs of visitors who eagerly await and then applaud the striking sunset over the water.

To continue the tour of Menemsha, retrace your route on Basin Road and turn right, toward Menemsha Basin. The Galley, situated across from the basin on the right side of the road, serves lobster rolls along with a variety of sandwiches and soft ice cream.

Menemsha Basin provides a safe harbor for fishing vessels that unload bluefish, tuna, halibut, schrod, bass, swordfish, and lobster. The Basin originally was a natural tidal creek that supplied an erratic flow of water into Menemsha Pond. In order to create this busy harbor, workers had to pile rocks at the entrance to the basin and repeatedly dredge the bottom.

Turn right to walk the length of **Dutcher Dock,** past the Coast Guard Station, to note the nets, lobster pots, rigging, buoys and shacks--colorful testimony to this active fishing community. If you look west across the channel, you'll discover **Lobsterville**, the most important fishing village on Martha's Vineyard 100 hundred years ago.

To continue your ride, return to the main road, ascend the steep grade and turn right onto the Menemesha Cross Road.

10. Pedal 1 mile on the cross road. At **Beetlebung Corner** (also Chilmark Center, comprising the town hall, firehouse and the Methodist Church), turn left onto Middle Road.

"Beetlebung" is the island name for the tupelo tree. A cluster of tupelos grow on the south corner of Middle Road.

11. Remain on this hilly road for 4.3 miles. Middle Road is my personal favorite because it's shaded, uncrowded, and so picturesque. As I'm pumping up the hills, I enjoy looking at the Tiasquam River flowing by farms nestled near its banks. After each ascent, I love being rewarded by a panoramic view of the Vineyard's south coast.

Hiking opportunities abound along this road: **Fulling Mill Brook Preserve** (Trip 14) is located on the right, 1.3 miles from Beetlebung Corner. A road to **Peaked Hill Reservation** (Trip 15) is located almost directly across Middle Road from the preserve. **Middle Road Sanctuary** (Trip 13) sits on the right, a half-mile from Fulling Mill Brook.

12. At the T intersection with Music Street, turn right toward the center of West Tisbury, a town that continues to reflect its origins as a rural farming village.

13. Turn left at the junction with South Road.

If you need refreshment, ahead on the left lies the inviting porch of **Alley's General Store.** Upon entering Alley's, whose sign boasts "Dealers in Almost Everything," one is transported a hundred years to the pre-supermarket era when the general store supplied provisions and was the center of a community's social life.

Back Alley's, at the rear of the parking lot, is a café that sells take-out food.

Across the street lies the **Field Gallery,** whose delightful sculptures by Tom Maley scamper over the grounds.

14. At the fork, stay right, remaining on the Edgartown-West Tisbury Road for the 9-mile return to Edgartown.

Almost immediately, on your left, is the picturesque Mill Pond, often surrounded by ducks and swans patiently waiting for generous travelers to stop and feed them.

15. The bike path/sidewalk begins on the left side just after the pond. When this bike path ends, look to your left for a dirt path that ascends to a bike path that runs through the State Forest.

16. Go right, in an easterly direction, on the path. Although this path is generally straight, it takes an abrupt turn into the forest in order to bypass a wedge of privately owned land.

17. Continue east, passing the airport and crossing Barnes Road. At this point, bikers returning to Oak Bluffs or Vineyard Haven should turn left on Barnes Road, and ride 2.4 miles to the "blinker."

Edgartown cyclists should remain on the Edgartown-West Tisbury Road.

18. Proceed 1.7 miles to the end of the old bike path and bear left onto a newer section.

19. Pedal 0.1 mile and cross the road to continue on the bike path for 2.3 miles.

Morning Glory Farm sits on the right, 1.5 miles after the bike path crosses the Edgartown-West Tisbury Road. This farm stand sells fresh produce as well as home-baked pastries and also offers an excellent salad bar.

20. After the bike path ends, remain on the Edgartown-West Tisbury Road for 0.3 mile to Cannonball Park.

TRIP 28
AQUINNAH AND LOBSTERVILLE LOOP

Rating: Difficult

Distance: 42 miles round trip from the ferry terminal in Vineyard Haven; add 3 miles to visit Lobsterville.

Food and Drink: Vineyard Haven: Stop & Shop Supermarket, Black Dog Bakery; Chilmark: Chilmark Chocolates, Chilmark Store; Aquinnah: shops at the top of the cliffs; West Tisbury: Cronig's Down Island Market.

Restrooms: Vineyard Haven: In the Steamship Authority Terminal; Aquinnah: Portable toilets at the entrance to the beach and in a small building adjacent to the parking lot (fee).

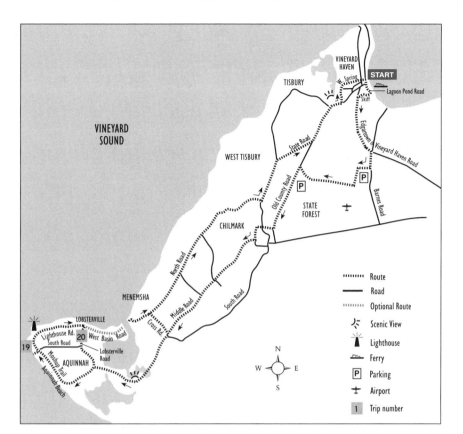

The trip from Vineyard Haven to Aquinnah and back, spanning twenty-one miles in each direction, is the most strenuous but also the most rewarding ride in this book.

Trip Description

The rolling terrain creates the strain,
But don't complain; there is much to gain
From the scenery, which, in the main,
Does, indeed, lessen the pain!

In order to reach Aquinnah, you must bike through Chilmark, whose rolling hills and landscape resemble northern New England. When you reach remote Aquinnah, you will discover a village very different from other island towns. Many Wampanoags have settled in Aquinnah, and the town reflects this heritage. Most Wampanoag tribe members no longer earn their living

The clay ridges of Gay Head Cliffs.

farming and fishing as did their ancestors. Some are now store proprietors selling American Indian items in the shops on top of the Gay Head Cliffs.

Additional rewards for climbing those rolling hills are relaxing on Aquinnah Beach, viewing the colorful cliffs from below and then ascending to the top for the panorama that's drawing all those tour buses (see Trip 19).

The Route

Edgartown Bikers: Go west on the Edgartown-Vineyard Haven Road to the "blinker"/4-way stop at Barnes Road. Turn left and pick up these directions at No. 6.

Oak Bluffs Bikers: Follow the directions in the West Tisbury South Loop in Trip 25 through No. 6, and then continue on the Edgartown-Vineyard Haven Road to the "blinker" at Barnes Road. Turn left and pick up the directions in this trip at No. 6.

1. From the Steamship Authority Terminal in Vineyard Haven, walk your bike through the traffic up Union Street to Water Street, the first road on the left.

2. Turn left on Water Street.

The Black Dog Bakery on the left side of Water Street sells breads and pastries, in addition to sandwiches and soups. The Stop & Shop, on the right side, sells typical supermarket fare along with prepared food at their deli counter.

3. At the "Five Corners" Intersection, walk your bike straight across State Road to Lagoon Pond Road.

4. Take the first right onto Skiff Avenue and ascend the hill. (Training for higher, longer hills ahead!)

5. Follow Skiff to the T intersection with the Edgartown-Vineyard Haven Road. Turn left. Pedal 0.4 mile to the bike path.

6. Continue on the bike path for 1.7 miles until you reach the intersection with Barnes Road, which boasts a "blinker," the only traffic light on the island. Turn right at the "blinker" onto the bike path on the right side of Barnes Road.

7. Pedal 0.5 mile in the direction of the airport. Turn right onto the bike path heading into the Manuel F. Correllus State Forest. The path heads west for 0.5 mile and then veers sharply south for another 0.5 mile.

8. *Don't miss* the right turn onto a bike path that leads to West Tisbury. This path cuts through the forest for 2 miles.

9. Turn left before the barrier, which prevents vehicles other than bikes from using the path, onto a path that emerges from the left.

10. Bike for 1 mile until the path no longer parallels County Road and begins to veer south. Bear right onto the side path to County Road. Continue biking south on County Road.

11. Remain on County Road for 1 mile. Upon reaching the Granary Gallery on the left, a popular art gallery that carries pictures by island artists and photographers, turn right onto Scotchman's Lane (you may not find a street sign, which is typical of the island's rural areas).

12. Stay on this road for 0.7 mile, crossing the intersection with State Road and then passing the Agricultural Society Hall and Grounds, site of the annual agricultural fair that takes place the third weekend in August. After riding by a fenced wildlife refuge on your right, turn right onto the first paved street, Middle Road. Again, there may not be a street sign.

13. Remain on scenic Middle Road, ascending and descending for 4.3 miles until you reach Chilmark Center at the junction of Middle Road, Menemsha Cross Road, and South Road. Go straight through the intersection onto South Road toward Aquinnah.

The name of this intersection, Beetlebung Corner, describes how the first English settlers used the wood from tupelo trees, which grow in the left corner of Middle Road. They formed the tupelo's tough, dense wood into "beetles," or wooden mallets, and "bungs," or corks for plugging the holes in barrels. The colonists then used the "beetles" to hammer "bungs" into barrels.

If you need to refill your water bottle, you'll find a spigot to the right of the Chilmark Store, located on the right side of South Road just past Beetle-bung Corner. This shop sells a variety of foodstuffs, but specializes in pizza and iced coffee drinks.

For a serious energy boost, head for Chilmark Chocolates, just down the road on the right. When you enter the shop, you will be dazzled by the array of confections. Make sure you look through the window on your right to watch the candy-making process, performed by people with a wide variety of abilities. Biking the many miles to Aquinnah ensures a guilt-free stop at this unique establishment.

14. Remain on this arduous but scenic stretch of road for 3.5 miles.

One mile from Chilmark Chocolates is **Nashaquitsa Overlook**, a turnoff that offers a spectacular view of Nashaquitsa Pond, which flows into Menemsha Pond (Trip 44). Look to the right for Menemsha, a fishing village nestled next to the ocean. If you are blessed with a clear day, you can peer out across the water to the Elizabeth Islands, lying between Vineyard Sound and Buzzards Bay.

15. Turn left onto Moshup Trail. Follow Moshup Trail for 3 miles to the public beach on the left. If you wish to stop to swim or stroll by the ocean, head down the boardwalk and park your bike in the rack on the beach.

16. To continue the ride, proceed up the road to the lighthouse and cliffs, the destination of all the tour buses that have whizzed by. A bike rack is located next to the parking lot. See Trip 19 for information on the beach and Gay Head Cliffs.

17. The return trip cuts across the north side of the island to the Lobsterville section of Aquinnah. From the cliffs, pedal back toward the parking lot, and turn left onto Lighthouse Road. This 2-mile stretch parallels South Road, offering panoramic views of Dogfish Bay.

One hundred years ago, before the creation of Menemsha Harbor, **Lobsterville** was the most important fishing village on Martha's Vineyard. Ships from New York made daily visits to purchase fish and lobster. Now the village no longer exists and the area is used for beaching, fishing, and enjoying the views of Menemsha Harbor and Menemsha Pond.

You can choose to take an optional 3-mile side visit and/or bike ferry trip to Menemsha by continuing past the junction with Lobsterville Road and proceeding for another 1.5 miles through Lobsterville to Menemsha Basin. From there you can take the bike ferry to Menemsha (steep fee but eliminates 6.8 miles and is available only during summer) and pick up the directions at No. 21, or you can turn around, return on the same road and continue to follow the directions.

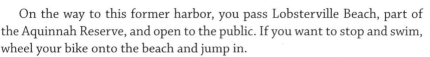

On the way to this former harbor, you pass Lobsterville Beach, part of the Aquinnah Reserve, and open to the public. If you want to stop and swim, wheel your bike onto the beach and jump in.

Cranberry Lands, across from the beach, are covered with wild roses, bayberry bushes and cranberries.

The road ends at Memesha Basin. Across the channel sits the village of Menemsha, a thriving fishing port, and home to many of the vessels whose owners continue to earn their living from the sea. If you look north across Vineyard Sound, you'll see Naushon, the largest Elizabeth Island.

18. To return to South Road, retrace your route on West Basin Road until you reach Lobsterville Road. Turn left onto Lobsterville Road and climb for 0.7 mile.

If you want to do a short hike, you can stop at Gay Head Moraine, on the right 0.3 mile ahead (Trip 20).

19. At the intersection with South Road, turn left and proceed 4.9 miles to Beetlebung Corner.

The first right turn off South Road leads to the new Wampanoag Tribal Office.

20. At Beetlebung Corner, turn left on Menemsha Cross Road.

21. At the junction with North Road, turn right, following the signs to Vineyard Haven. Remain on this road for 10 miles until you reach West Spring Street in Vineyard Haven.

North Road is my preferred return route because it is flatter and its many commercial establishments offer good excuses to stop.

22. Turn left on West Spring Street, the street after the Lake Tashmoo Overlook.

23. Follow West Spring as it bends around. Bear left at the fork and then bend right, keeping the school on the right. Remain on Spring, which runs into Main Street in Vineyard Haven Center.

24. Turn left on Main.

25. Turn right onto Union Street, which returns to the Steamship Authority Wharf.

3

Off-Road Biking on Martha's Vineyard

Martha's Vineyard is an off-road biker's paradise. Because of all the conservation land, you can literally bike on trails from one end of the island to the other. The Martha's Vineyard Land Bank has made it a priority to purchase land that adjoins other conservation land so people will have the opportunity to bike or hike all over the island. In most of the following off-road trips I have linked properties and have given you the option of connecting to other areas.

Safety and Etiquette

In order to preserve the areas open to off-road bikers, please follow these rules:

1. Keep off trails posted with No Biking signs.

2. Stay on the trails. Never create new ones.

3. Do not ride between January 1 and April 30.

4. Practice low-impact cycling: Dismount in areas where your tires will leave an imprint, such as wetlands, moist stream beds or on certain soils after a heavy rain; avoid skidding when ascending or descending steep slopes.

5. Always relinquish the right of way to other trail users.

6. When meeting horseback riders, dismount until the horse has passed.

7. Ride in control.

8. Alert other trail users if you intend to pass.

9. Do not ride alone.

TRIP 29
PENNYWISE PRESERVE AND DR. FISHER ROAD

Location: Edgartown
Rating: Easy but with some sandy sections.
Distance: 7 miles

Take this route across newly cut trails and ancient ways.

Directions
Heading toward Edgartown on the Edgartown/Vineyard Haven Road, proceed 2.5 miles from the "blinker"/stop-sign intersection with Barnes Road and turn right onto 18th Street. Proceed 0.25 mile to the preserve.

Trip Description
The combination of a new Land Bank property with an ancient way allows for an exploration of the interior of the more-developed eastern end of the island. Pennywise Preserve is a 118-acre woodland that connects to the historic Dr. Fisher Road. The entire length of the "ancient way" was constructed in the mid-1800s by Dr. Daniel Fisher, a wealthy Edgartown resident, to carry grain from his gristmill in West Tisbury to his home in Edgartown. The return route is especially scenic as it passes through a low sandy area created by glacial melting and travels along a newly cut path around the private Vineyard Golf Course.

The Route

1. Ride through the parking area and go left between two large boulders. Go straight, passing a bench, conveniently located for snacking or resting before the ride. The trail crosses through a meadow and then reaches an old narrow path, named Three Cornered Rock Road.

2. Turn left, remaining in the meadow, onto this sandy path (gearing down or pedaling on the edge of the path helps on sand).

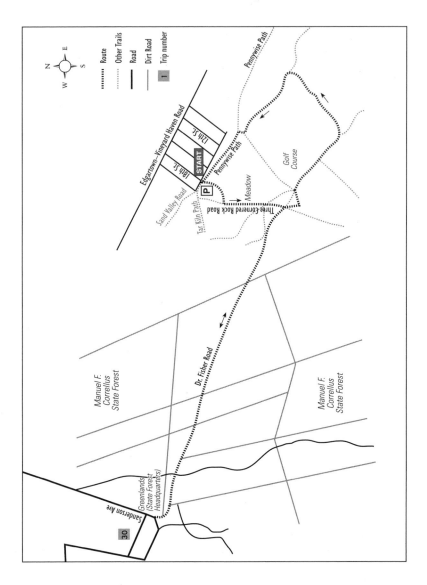

The trail proceeds through the typical Vineyard forest with oak trees and an undergrowth of huckleberry and blueberry bushes (handy if you are hungry).

3. After having gone almost 1 mile, you reach a wide dirt road piled high with fertilizer to be used for the private golf course just ahead. Make a hard right to access the Dr. Fisher Road, which is marked by cedar stakes on each side of the trail.

For 0.6 mile the trail is fairly level but then it runs behind a housing de-velopment and the terrain changes from rocky to sandy to solid ground.

The intersection with a fire lane indicates that the trail has entered the State Forest. Now the conditions of the path will vary depending on how diligent the workers have been in maintaining the trail. Because this section of the island is sandplain, the trails tend to be sandy so it's best to ride after a rainstorm, which makes the sand firmer to ride on.

4. After riding for 3 miles the trail ends at a dirt road. Turn right.

5. Continue on the road until you reach a Y intersection. Bear right and head for the barricade that prevents cars from entering.

Decision: Turn around and retrace your route on Dr. Fisher Road to ac-cess the path around the golf course and complete the loop in Pennywise Path Reserve or continue on to trip 30, which begins at this spot.

6. To return on Dr. Fisher Road, go back through the barricade and bear left on the dirt road.

7. Turn left onto Dr. Fisher Road. Follow the trail back to the point where you made the turn from Three Cornered Rock Road.

8. Instead of making the turn, cross the dirt road, passing a huge mound of organic fertilizer to be used on the golf course, turn right onto another dirt road and IMMEDIATELY turn left onto a partially hidden single-track trail.

Remain on this trail for 0.3 mile as it runs by the golf course and crosses through a section of mini-scrub oak trees. When the golf course was being con-structed, the builders were very careful not to disrupt this rare ecosystem.

The size of the trees indicates that this area is what is referred to as a **frost bottom**, a low sandy area created by glacial melting. When the last ice sheet began to melt and recede 15,000 years ago, it dropped millions of tons of sand it had picked up during its slow southern flow. Much of the Vineyard was formed from runoff of this sandy residue, as you probably have noticed when trying to pedal on these sandy trails.

The glacier carved away this lower elevation, which can be considerably hotter or colder than the surrounding terrain. As a result, it experiences ear-lier and later frosts than the higher ground. Only certain species can live in a microclimate with temperature drops that destroy early spring growth. The hardy **scrub oak** is one type of plant that manages to survive under these conditions, but grows much smaller than normal.

9. Pick up the path on the other side of the paved entrance road to the golf course and proceed about 250 feet.

10. Turn left on this newly cut trail and enjoy views of the Scottish-inspired link-style golf course. Remain on this trail for 0.4 mile.

11. Turn left onto a dirt road.

12. The road immediately bears right but you go straight on the path that continues to border the golf course.

13. The path stops. Take a right, leaving the golf course.

14. Upon reaching a dirt road with an oak tree directly in front of you, turn left onto Pennywise Path. (Don't expect to see any road sign.)

15. Follow this road which can be quite sandy in parts, but also dirt- and pine-needle-covered, until you reach 18th Street where the ride began.

TRIP 30
STATE FOREST TO THIMBLE FARM

Location: West Tisbury
Rating: Mostly easy with a few tricky sections.
Distance: 8 miles

The variety of terrain makes this my favorite off-road ride.

Directions
From Vineyard Haven: follow the Edgartown-Vineyard Haven Road for 2.7 miles to Martha's Vineyard Regional High School. Turn right onto Sanderson Avenue, just to the left (east) of the school. Follow Sanderson for 1 mile. The route begins on the right across from the fire road barrier gate (at the point where the road turns right). The forest supervisor office is ahead. You can park your car on the side of the road.

Trip Description
This loop ride begins in the Manuel F. Correllus State Forest, links to the Greenlands, rides through Little Duarte's Pond Preserve and circles around Thimble Farm. You also have the opportunity to connect to two other off-road rides so if you wish, you can pedal on dirt all day.

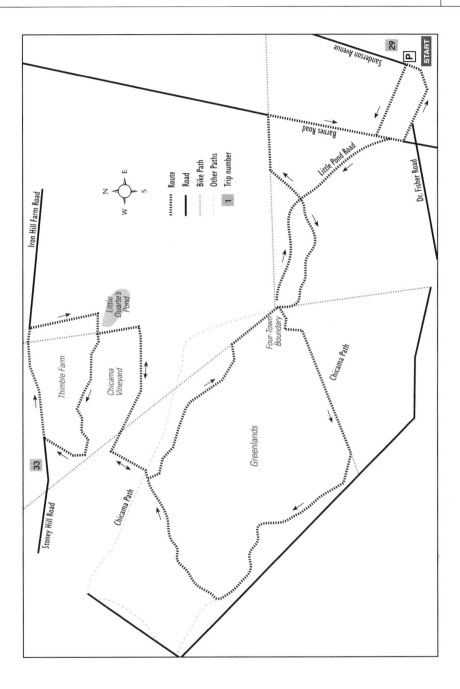

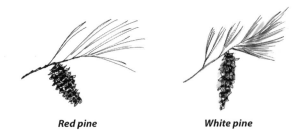

Red pine   *White pine*

The Route

1. With your back to the barrier gate on the left (east) side of the road, turn right and pedal a few hundred feet.

2. Look on the left side for a large boulder blocking a path heading into a pine forest. Proceed 0.2 mile on this straight, level pine-needle-covered path.

3. At T-intersection, turn left and go down the hill to the paved road, which is the main entrance to the Manuel F. Correllus State Forest.

In 1908, the Commonwealth of Massachusetts paid one dollar plus back taxes for 612 acres of centrally located land to use as a sanctuary for the endangered heath hen. However, the heath hen did not fare any better on the Vineyard than anywhere else. None have been seen in the forest for more than 60 years. In 1925, the state began to buy much of the surrounding land. Within two years the forest had grown to its present 4,343 acres.

Due to frequent fires, which retarded tree growth, the forest remained a sandplain grassland habitat until 1934. At that time, the Civilian Conservation Corps planted red pine, white pine, and spruce trees. Unfortunately, many red pines, which thrive in colder northern regions, adjusted poorly to the Vineyard's more temperate climate. The red pines became stressed and fell prey to disease, primarily the fungus *Diplodea pinea*. As you bike through the forest you will see dead tree trunks, remnants of this species of pine. The white pine and spruce trees are better adapted to this climate and continue to thrive.

Manuel F. Correllus began working in the forest in 1938. He became supervisor ten years later, and remained in that position until 1987. In 1988, in recognition of fifty years of dedication to his work, the forest was named the Manuel F. Correllus State Forest.

4. Turn right onto the paved road, passing the State Forest sign.

5. Cross Barnes Road and follow the short dirt path to the paved bike trail.

6. Turn left on the bike trail and proceed 0.1 mile until you reach a barricade on your left and wide dirt road on your right.

Taking a relaxing ride on the bike path in the Manuel F. Corellus State Forest.

7. Turn right onto the road.

8. Proceed about 200 feet and turn right onto the path that leads into the forest. This path twists and turns until it reaches an open area with many dead tree limbs.

9. Turn left to find the path that heads back into the forest. This wider and straighter path leads into a meadow. Remain on this path until you reach a confusing jumble of paths with a pine tree in the center.

10. Take the path on the far left. Now in the meadow, the trail changes from wide and sandy to narrow and grassy as you bike for 0.4 mile amid a bounty of colorful wildflowers.

You may also notice many dead oak trees, a result of a three-year infestation of defoliating caterpillars that caused widespread stress to the oak trees. Throughout the island, hundreds of acres of oak trees died.

11. When the trail starts to make a loop, leave the meadow and head onto the paved bike trail.

12. Turn right and proceed about 200 feet.

13. When the bike path makes a sharp right (a white-topped post with an A on it marks the spot), turn left into the Margaret K. Littlefield Greenlands, land owned by the town of West Tisbury but whose trails were recently cut by the Martha's Vineyard Land Bank.

The name of this spot is Four Town Bound as the boundaries of Edgartown, Oak Bluffs, West Tisbury, and Tisbury join here.

14. Upon entering the Greenlands, take the trail on the left. Proceed 0.5 mile first through a scrub oak woodland and then through a section with taller oaks.

15. At the fork in the trail, bear right. A small orange blaze indicates that you are still on the orange-blazed trail.

16. Proceed 0.6 mile (2.6 total) to a fork in the trail, bear right (a tall oak tree sits in the center of the fork).

In 0.1 mile a bench under a large oak tree invites you to stop and rest.

17. After another 0.7 mile, you reach another fork. Go left.

18. Turn right onto a dirt road and make a quick left onto the continuation of the orange-blazed trail.

19. Cross another dirt road where you will see a Land Bank sign stating "Trail easement to Little Duarte's Pond 0.5 mile." This green-blazed trail runs beside a split-rail fence containing horses (which are probably responsible for the souvenirs along the trail).

Remain on the trail as it ascends and steeply descends.

20. Cross another road.

Stakes for the vines from the former Chicama Vineyard stand on the left.

21. Continue on the road that skirts the vineyard for 200 feet and then turn right at the post with the green arrow (3.2 miles).

22. Cross one dirt road. When you reach a second one, turn right. A reassuring Land Bank green blaze is ahead.

23. Remain on the road for 0.3 mile until you reach a prominent Land Bank sign announcing "Little Duarte's Pond." Turn left (3.6 miles) onto a more challenging trail. Ride down the hill to a wood-chipped path and a sign noting "Sensitive habitat." The path swings around, allowing a view of the pond.

If you wish, you can park your bike and stroll down the path for a better view. In summer, the edge of the pond is decorated with the cone-shaped bright pink flowers of **steeplebush spirea**.

Continue across a wooden-plank bridge until you reach the Thimble Farm Loop.

24. At the fence and T intersection, turn left (3.8 miles).

25. Pedal for 0.5 mile on this grassy path that borders the farm until you reach the red-blazed Land Bank easement signs. Leave the farmland.

Thimble Farm is owned privately but the Martha's Vineyard Land Bank owns the development rights and has stipulated that the fields themselves be used only for agriculture. The Land Bank also owns a trail easement around three sides of the property.

Decision: You can connect with Wapatequa Woods Preserve and Tisbury Meadow Preserve by turning left onto the smooth dirt farm road and then turning right onto bumpy Stoney Hill Road. Pedaling 0.2 mile will take you to the entrance of Wapatequa Woods Preserve. You can follow the directions in Trip 33 or you can proceed to No. 26 and continue.

26. Turn right onto the dirt farm road. Follow it for 0.5 mile until you reach the dirt road that borders the northern edge of the farm.

27. Turn right onto this road which leads to Little Duarte's Pond.

28. Follow the road until the end for another view of the pond and then backtrack to take a left onto the Thimble Farm Loop.

29. Proceed 0.1 mile and turn left at the Trail Easement to Greenlands sign, now back on the path that you biked earlier.

At this steep section, you can cross-train by walking your bike while admiring the variety of groundcover: grayish **reindeer lichen**, bright green **haircap moss**, and dark green **bearberry** growing alongside the trail.

30. Turn right onto the dirt road. Proceed 0.3 mile until you spot the Private Road, No Public Access sign.

31. Turn left onto the trail.

32. Proceed 0.6 mile until you come to a V intersection. Bear left onto the remaining section of the orange-blazed Greenlands trail.

Here you'll find relaxed riding through a typical Vineyard forest with oak trees above and an understory of **huckleberry bushes.**

33. Now back onto the paved bike path. Turn right.

34. Turn left to ride on the opposite side of the meadow that you rode earlier.

35. While in the meadow continue bearing left until you reach the paved bike path.

36. To return to your starting point on Sanderson Road, turn right on the bike path.

37. Turn right again to access the bike path heading south.

38. Remain on the bike path for 0.4 mile until you reach the paved entrance to the State Forest. Turn left.

39. Follow this road back to the barricade.

If you wish to continue biking off-road, go to Trip 29, Pennywise Preserve and Dr. Fisher Road, and pick up the directions at No. 6.

TRIP 31
THREE PONDS RESERVATION

Location: Chappaquiddick

Rating: Easy to moderate (The path to Hickory Cove is steep.)

Distance: 4.3 miles

Restrooms: Chappaquiddick Community Center, which is adjacent to Brine's Pond Preserve.

Food and Drink: Chappy General Store, on Chappaquiddick Road, 0.5 miles east of Brine's Pond Preserve.

Fees: Chappy Ferry. At the time of publication, bikers pay $6.00 and drivers pay $12.00 plus $3.00 for each additional passenger for a round-trip ride.

Ride this trail through four Land Bank properties: North Farm, Hickory Cove, Brine's Pond Preserve, and Chappy Five Corners Preserve.

Directions

From the Chappy Ferry, proceed 1.3 miles to North Neck Road. (The street name is etched on a wooden post.) The entrance road forms an upside-down V.

Trip Description

This ride visits three ponds of varying sizes: tiny Buttonbush Pond hidden away in North Farm, scenic Brine's Pond which features an island of beetle-bung trees perched in its center, and Cape Poge Bay, one of the largest bod-

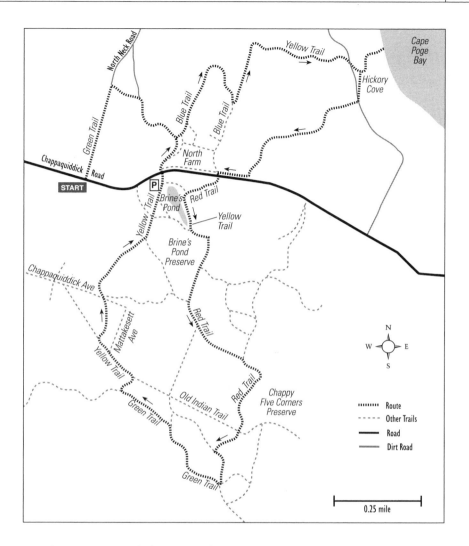

ies of water on Martha's Vineyard. Make sure you bring mosquito repellent along with a bathing suit and water shoes if you want to cool off in Cape Poge Bay.

The Route

1. At North Neck Road, you have a choice of whether to ride for a quarter-mile on a dirt road or on a path. The path begins on the left side of the road and after 0.1 mile, crosses to the right side. Because the path on the right side is significantly higher than the road, be prepared to hoist your bike.

2. If on the road look on the right for a large boulder with a North Farm Land Bank sign and a wide path heading into the woods.

3. Remain on this path for 0.2 mile. The North Farm sign appears near a large beautiful oak tree which sits in front of a farmhouse.

Buttonbush Pond is hidden behind the house. The trail then runs by farmland, which formerly covered most of Chappaquiddick during the island's early years when colonists used the land to graze sheep and cows.

At the T intersection, turn left, following the North Farm Loop trail.

4. Proceed 0.25 mile to another T intersection. Turn left at the sign toward Hickory Cove.

Whereas most of the route is mellow riding, this narrow path ascends, descends, twists, and turns as it runs through a pine forest and oak woodland.

Cross a dirt road and pedal past a stake with the Land Bank logo.

Proceed 0.2 mile and continue straight, crossing another dirt road and then riding through a meadow before entering another woodland.

5. After riding a total of 0.6 mile on this path, you arrive at Hickory Cove. The Land Bank signboard and parking lot is on the left. The dirt road leads to the boat launching area. A sandier section of the beach lies to the right of this rockier section.

If you would rather just contemplate this pristine setting, turn right and head for the bench sitting in the middle of a meadow that is often covered with wildflowers. Enjoy the view of Cape Poge Bay, which is featured in the paddling section of this book. Only an occasional fishing boat or kayaker ventures into this remote and undeveloped area.

6. To return, follow the same trail, while elevating your heart rate with the short steep hills.

7. Now back at North Farm, turn left at the T intersection to complete the loop.

The Brine's Pond sign appears 0.2 mile from the Hickory Cove turn-off.

8. Continue on the trail until you reach Chappaquiddick Road. Turn left and immediately cross the road as the entrance path to Brine's Pond is well-hidden.

9. Turn right onto the path to Brine's Pond Preserve. The Land Bank signboard is set back from the road.

10. Proceed on this red-blazed path until you reach Brine's Pond. A trail marked by yellow blazes skirts the edge of the pond. Turn left.

Brine's Pond.

The Chappaquiddick Community Center is located on the opposite side of the pond.

The Martha's Vineyard Land Bank has cut back the foliage to allow a good view of lily pads surrounding a grove of beetlebung trees. Beetlebung is the Vineyard name for the **tupelo** tree. Early settlers used its dense wood for wooden "beetles" or mallets which drove the "bungs" or corks that were used to plug barrel holes.

11. Remain on the yellow trail until you come to a T intersection. Turn left onto the Red Trail. (A red blaze is tacked to a tree but is hidden by foliage.)

If you are biking in July and seek a succulent snack, watch for **blueberries** growing on the low bushes beside the trail.

Mellow biking now for 0.4 mile on this wide, pine-needle-covered trail.

12. At the 3-way intersection bear left, continuing to follow the Red Trail and the tan and green Cross-Chappy signs.

13. After proceeding 0.2 mile, cross the dirt road and turn right, watching on the left for the Chappy Five Corners sign and the red blazes on the trees. The path leads to the Land Bank Chappy Five Corners signpost.

The trail leads to a meadow. When I was there I spotted a red-tailed hawk swooping around searching for an unsuspecting rodent.

14. Turn left, following the red/green-blazed trail.

15. Upon reaching the meadow, turn right at the big oak tree, now watching for green blazes on the trees.

The increased numbers of mosquitoes indicate that you are now in a wetland environment.

16. Upon reaching the yellow/green blazed-trail, turn left to complete the loop to Brine's Pond. Thankfully, you have returned to a drier environment consisting of the usual oak woodland with an understory of huckleberry bushes.

17. Turn right onto a dirt road (actually, a driveway).

18. Take the next left onto Old Indian Trail Road (no sign).

19. Bear right at the fork in the road.

20. Watch for a red-blazed Land Bank sign on the right side of the road. Turn right, following the path as it travels over the remains of a stone wall.

21. Now back on the Yellow Trail, continue bearing left as the path returns to the meadow containing Brine's Pond. Remain on the path until it ends at Chappaquiddick Road.

TRIP 32
POUCHA POND RESERVATION

Location: Chappaquiddick

Rating: Easy, but the trail through the salt marsh is often muddy.

Distance: 1.8 miles

Restrooms: Located at Mytoi, East Beach (Trip 5) and Wasque Reservation (Trip 6).

Food and Drink: Chappy General Store, located 2.2 miles from the ferry landing and 1.6 miles from the reservation.

Fees: Chappy Ferry. At the time of publication, bikers pay $6.00 and drivers pay $12.00 plus $3.00 for each additional passenger for a round-trip ride.

This short ride offers a variety of views.

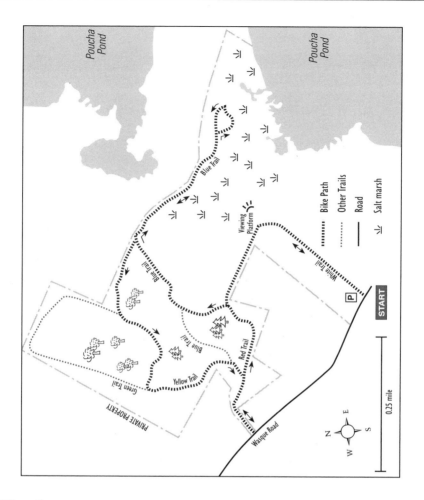

Directions

The reservation is 4.1 miles from the Chappy Ferry. Follow Chappaquiddick Road to Wasque Road and turn left. Proceed 0.8 mile to the entrance on the left side of the road.

Trip Description

While biking around Chappaquiddick, stop at Poucha Pond Reservation for some mellow riding on pine-needle-covered trails that wind through open fields and woods. Pause at the viewing platform to admire the vista all the way to Nantucket. Cycle along a salt marsh to small islands in Poucha Pond, a body of water that extends from famous Dike Bridge to remote Wasque Point. Observe the many species of birds that feast on the abundant fin and

Egrets foraging for food in the salt marsh.

shellfish in this marshy pond. Take along mosquito repellent. To swim, head for Wasque Reservation or East Beach.

The Route

1. From the parking area, proceed down a wide level trail 0.2 mile to the viewing platform on the right. On a clear day you can see as far as Nantucket, and on most days you have a view of Nantucket Sound and East Beach.

2. Continue bearing right through this typical Vineyard pitch pine forest.

Notice the small pine trees growing beside the trail. Whenever land is cleared, the cut pines quickly reappear because their large root systems lie close to the surface, waiting for enough open space to sprout.

After leaving the pine forest, the path winds through a woodland filled with oak trees. Years ago, this section was probably inhabited by pine trees. However, once the oak trees took hold, they overshadowed the pines, causing them to weaken and die. This process of succession often reveals how many years have elapsed since the land was farmed. The type of vegetation indicates each stage in the process. Red cedar trees are often the first to sprout in open fields, followed by woody shrubs like huckleberry and blueberry. Pitch pine trees follow, and the last variety of tree in the order of succession is the oak.

3. At the next T intersection, turn right onto the Blue Trail which leads to the salt marsh.

The closer you get to the water, the more gnarled and deformed the trees, victims of the strong winds that bombard this side of the island.

The **groundsel tree**, also called the high tide bush, grows at the edge of the marsh. It's easier to spot this shrub in autumn when the seeds on the female plant mature into small, white, feathery clusters.

This trail leads to several pond and marsh lookouts, excellent vantage points to spot **common** and **least terns** fishing the shallow water for minnows. You also may see **great black-backed** and **herring gulls** that are responsible for the broken shells you see on the ground. The gulls pull the shellfish out of the water, fly into the air, and drop the shellfish on the hard ground. The gulls then swoop down and yank the contents out of the broken shells.

Three varieties of herons feed in the marsh: the **short green heron**, the **great blue heron** and the **black-crowned night heron**. You may also spot marsh hawks and short-eared owls. The last time I was in Poucha Pond Reservation, I saw at least ten bright white **great egrets** looking around for food. These large birds are actually herons; both great egrets and great blue herons have long pointed yellow bills.

These birds are drawn to the salt marsh to feed on fin fish and shellfish that thrive in this nutrient-rich environment. An acre of salt marsh yields an estimated 242 pounds of nutrients, mostly in the form of vegetation, which, in turn, feeds about 300 pounds of shellfish. Tides carry nutritious organic matter from the salt marsh into ponds and out to the ocean where other species of fish feed on it.

4. Follow the trail as it goes from one island to the other.

5. Bear right to take the loop that skirts the salt marsh.

6. After completing the loop, turn left to retrace your route on the Blue Trail through the marsh.

If you are hiking in late summer or early fall you will see the marsh decorated with tiny purple flowers. This small delicate plant is called **sea lavender**. Another fall flower is **seaside goldenrod,** which produces bright

Groundsel tree

Egret

yellow flowers that line the edge of the marsh. The narrow channels you see cutting through the marsh are for mosquito control.

Two varieties of grasses growing here are **cord grass** and **saltmarsh hay**. Cord grass is the pioneer plant of salt marshes. It starts to grow at the edges of bays or ponds, where it produces stiff broad leaves that die back at the end of each growing season. The continual yearly dying back yields a build-up of sediments necessary to support other plant species such as salt marsh hay, a thinner, floppier grass. This hay is so rich in nutrients that the island's early settlers shepherded their livestock all the way to this remote corner so their animals could graze.

7. Remain on the Blue Trail until the intersection with the Yellow Trail. Bear right onto the Yellow Trail, lined with more wind-battered oak trees.

8. Bear left on the Yellow Trail as it merges with an old cart path and passes Wasque Farm on the right. Remain on the Yellow Trail as the cart path bears right.

9. At the intersection with the Blue Trail, turn right to return to a former entrance to Poucha Pond Reservation. You are now 0.3 miles farther north on Wasque Road than from where you started.

History of Poucha Pond Reservation

During the last three hundred years, settlers of Chappaquiddick found many uses for this remote property. At one time Poucha Pond was open to the sea. Boats traveling by Martha's Vineyard's eastern shore used it as a harbor, but, by 1722, storms and tides had filled the opening with sand.

In 1845, a few landowners constructed a dike in order to control the flow of water into and out of the pond. Each winter they closed the dike's gates to prevent salt water from entering. In spring they opened the gates so the herring and shad could swim into the pond and deposit their eggs. Fishermen then caught the fish, which they pickled, salted, and shipped in barrels to New York.

During the nineteenth century the marsh, too, was put to good use. Farmers drove their livestock to graze on the nutritious marsh grass. They also were able to harvest as many as four barrels of wild cranberries per day from this bountiful wetland. Hunters were drawn to the marsh and pond because of the numerous migrating waterfowl that stopped to feed. Now the pond is seeded and thus produces scallops and clams, which attract the shorebirds.

TRIP 33
WAPATEQUA WOODS RESERVATION
TO TISBURY MEADOW PRESERVE

Location: Tisbury

Rating: Easy riding in Wapatequa Woods; more strenuous in
Tisbury Meadow.

Distance: 4 miles

**This trip provides a combination of mellow and challenging
off-road riding.**

Directions

Coming from Vineyard Haven on the Edgartown-Vineyard Haven Road, turn
right onto Stoney Hill Road, the last street *before* the "blinker"/stop sign
intersection with Barnes Road. Proceed 0.9 mile to the parking area and
trailhead on the right.

Trip Description

Easy to access and fun to ride, these two Land Bank properties include typical Vineyard woodlands, ancient dirt roads, and a large meadow. If you are
in need of an energy boost, you can stop to pick from the plentiful blueberry
and huckleberry bushes that line the trails.

The Route

1. From the parking area, pedal down the grassy path (referred to as the
Northern Trail) past a cluster of bright green **hay-scented ferns** and
through a scrub oak forest with an understory of huckleberry bushes, passing on the left the trail that runs to the west side of Stoney Hill Road.

The path, dotted with rocks and tree roots, merges with a dirt road. The
road veers off and the composition of the trail returns to dirt, rocks, and
tree roots.

2. The trail ends at a horse farm surrounded by an electrified fence. Turn
right and bike beside the fence. The trail leaves the farm and enters a
woodland.

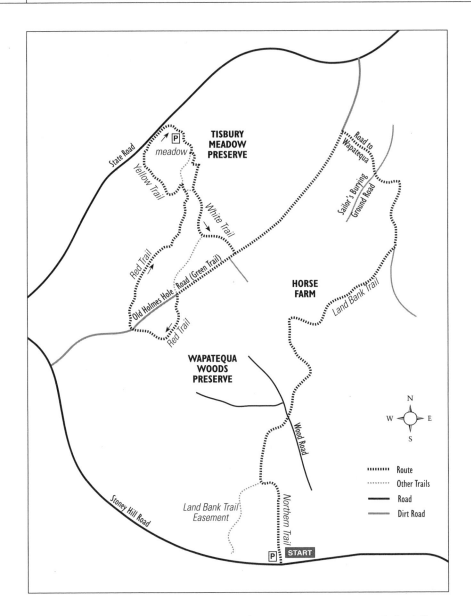

3. Just after the path ascends, you reach a T intersection. Turn left, following the green-blazed Land Bank logo.

4. The path again merges with an older trail and stops at a barricade. Go around the barricade and turn left.

5. Pass through another barricade and go straight, crossing a road, onto another road (referred to on the map as the "Road to Wapatequa," but don't expect to see a sign).

You will pass a log fence with granite posts on each side. Make sure you remain on the old road, not a grassy path. (You can tell the age of the road by how high the land is on each side; the lower the road in relation to the land, the more use it has had.)

6. Proceed onto a gravel road by making a quick left and then a quick right. You will know you are on the right road if you see telephone poles on the road.

7. Cross a paved road and continue straight on the path behind two large boulders. You are now on another "ancient way," Old Holmes Hole Road (no sign).

8. Continue bearing right on Holmes Hole Road for 0.5 mile, passing the trail with the green Land Bank blaze.

You'll notice that the Land Bank has kindly created side trails in order to avoid biking or walking on deep, rutted, muddy sections of the road.

9. You have entered Tisbury Meadow Preserve. Turn left on the red-blazed trail, which, strangely, is composed of both white sand and moss—moss is much easier to ride on than sand.

This steep, rocky, tree-rooted section enables you to cross-train by hauling your bike up the slope. It also allows you to pick and munch the **huckleberries** growing on the side of the trail.

10. When you reach a fork stay left to avoid an eroded section.

11. After 0.4 mile on the red-blazed trail, you reach a field which often has big-horned sheep grazing. Turn left and climb to the top of the field which is covered with **sumac** and **viburnum** bushes, **goldenrod**, and red-hued **velvet grass**.

12. Continue to circle the field until you reach the parking area for Tisbury Meadow Preserve. Go past the Martha's Vineyard Land Bank signboard until you reach the yellow-blazed trail.

13. Turn left onto this very steep, curvy, eroded trail.

14. Upon reaching a bench at the edge of the meadow, turn left to reenter the wooded section of the preserve.

15. Follow this steep, rocky trail and make another left onto the white-blazed trail.

16. Continue bearing left until you come to a T-intersection at Holmes Hole Road.

17. Turn left and remain on Holmes Hole Road for 0.2 mile until you reach the stone barricade.

18. Turn right, pedal 0.4 mile passing the Tisbury Water Works.

19. Turn right onto Wapatequa Road and continue 0.3 mile to a steel barricade.

20. Proceed 0.5 mile through the woods, pass the horse farm and turn left to return to Wapatequa Woods Preserve. Pedal 1 mile to the parking area.

21. If you wish to continue riding, turn to Trip 31 and pick up the directions at No. 25.

4

Paddling Martha's Vineyard

Paddling around the numerous ponds, coves, and bays on Martha's Vineyard can be a relaxing way to explore the island. A few precautions are in order: Be mindful of the wind and tides. Listen to the weather forecasts and check the tide charts, which appear weekly in Vineyard newspapers. A potentially relaxing paddle can turn into a stressful struggle if you have to battle current and wind. Usually the best time to paddle is in the morning. During July and August, southwest winds often increase in the mid-afternoon. When possible, I have tried to design the routes so the wind is at your back on the return.

Wear shoes to protect your feet from sharp shells, and a brimmed hat to save your head, face, and neck from the sun, which is doubly dangerous when reflected off the water. Slather on sun lotion, drink plenty of water, and don't forget a life vest.

It's very easy to lose perspective and direction when you are in the middle of a large body of water. So when embarking on a trip, make sure that you turn around and fix your location, using visual cues to guide you on your return.

Safety and Etiquette

To ensure a safe and comfortable paddling experience, consider the following safety tips:

- Know how to use your canoe or kayak. Small lakes and ponds are the perfect place for inexperienced paddlers to learn, but if you are new to the sport, you should have someone show you some basic paddling strokes and impress upon you how to enter and exit your boat. New paddlers should consider staying close to shore until they are more comfortable with their paddling skills. Luckily, some of the most interesting aspects of the trips are found along the shoreline.

- Stay off the water if thunderstorms are nearby. Lightning is a serious danger to boaters. If you hear a thunderstorm approaching, get off of the water immediately and seek shelter.
- Make sure everyone in your group is wearing a life jacket or personal flotation device (PFD) that fits properly and securely.
- Turn around *before* the members of your party start feeling tired. Paddling a few miles after your arms are spent already can make for cranky travelers. All of the trips in this book start and end at the same location, so you can easily turn around at any time.
- Give wildlife a wide berth. Lakes and ponds are much different than forests in that wildlife has less of an opportunity to hide from humans. The summer months see numerous people in the water, and the ducks, herons, and swans waste a good deal of energy just swimming or flying away from curious boaters. If you spot wildlife, remain still and quiet and let the animals decide whether or not to approach you. Use binoculars if you want a closer view.
- Sound carries a long way on the water, so try to keep your conversations quiet in order not to disturb other paddlers or residents.

TRIP 34
KATAMA BAY AND CALEB'S POND

Location: Edgartown

Rating: Moderate. A storm-created breach in what was once a barrier beach connecting Chappaquiddick to Edgartown has created a strong current. The southern side of the bay is fairly exposed, so paddling on a windy day can be challenging. Southwest winds generally increase around 3 P.M.

Distance: 3 miles long and 2.2 miles wide. Allow several hours to circle the bay and visit Caleb's Pond.

Paddle on a busy bay and a peaceful pond.

Directions
The boat launch is located in Edgartown on Edgartown Bay Road. Follow Katama Road south for 1.6 miles. Turn left onto Edgartown Bay Road. Proceed 0.8 mile, to the boat launch parking lot on the left.

Trip Description
If you are looking for visual variety, head for Katama Bay where grand Edgartown mansions overlook the water and luxurious yachts are anchored in the harbor. Across the bay from Edgartown, you'll find more relaxed paddling on tranquil Caleb's Pond. Boat traffic increases as you paddle north into Edgartown Harbor.

The Course

1. From the boat landing, head southwest into a small inlet called Mattakeset Bay. This section tends to be rather shallow, so don't get too close to shore, unless you wish to stop and swim.

2. Return to Katama Bay, paddling in a northeasterly direction. Be mindful of the current when you reach the center of the bay.

3. Upon reaching the eastern Chappaquiddick (Chappy) side, continue on a northward course, paddling through Edgartown's lower harbor.

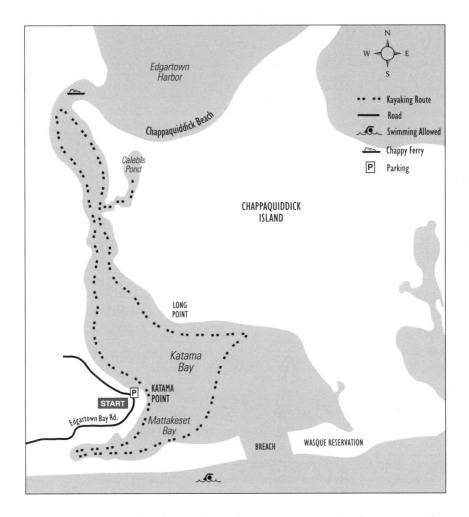

4. Remaining near the Chappy shore, keep your eye out for the narrow inlet into Caleb's Pond. Upon entering the pond, keep to the left and then hug the shore to prevent going aground in this shallow section. Once you enter the main pond, the water becomes deeper. The pond's calm water and isolation provide a striking contrast to the busy harbor.

5. If, after exploring the pond, you choose to continue paddling north, you will enter Edgartown's inner harbor.

During summer you will see two small car ferries shuttling between Edgartown and Chappaquiddick. Since each ferry is never more than a minute away from either side, they are named "On-Time."

A salt marsh near Katama Bay and Caleb's Pond.

6. At the ferry dock, make a U-turn to head south down the Edgartown side of the bay.

In the inner harbor, elegant old homes are perched by the water. As you progress south, you will have an excellent view of the newer mansions overlooking the bay.

Just before you reach the boat landing, you may spot **Katama Point**, a spit of land jutting out into the water. A small property owned by the Martha's Vineyard Land Bank, the preserve features a short trail, a small beach, and osprey.

TRIP 35
EEL POND AND EDGARTOWN OUTER HARBOR

Location: Edgartown

Rating: Moderate. Because some paddling is on the ocean (albeit on the calm north side), wind and current may be strong. If you continue into Edgartown Harbor, be alert to boat traffic and the wakes that follow.

Distance: The route described is approximately 6 miles (not including the optional explorations), but is easily shortened or lengthened, so you can paddle for an hour in Eel Pond or extend the trip for as long as your time and energy permit.

This trip offers action, accessibility, and options.

Directions
The boat launch is located off Braley's Way in Edgartown. From the intersection of Main Street and Pease's Point Way, head north on Pease's Point Way, following the signs to the Chappy Ferry. Remain on Pease's Point Way until it ends at Braley's Way. Turn left. Take the third right (look for a white picket fence). Follow the road to the boat launch area. After you unload your boat, you can park on either side of the road.

Trip Description
You may have to contend with boat traffic, which can be challenging and lively, but paddling in Edgartown's outer harbor offers many other less congested options. A northeasterly route allows exploration of Eel Pond, nestled in Lighthouse Beach's protective peninsula. Its shallow waters draw people and shorebirds seeking mollusks that inch along under the sand. You'll experience relaxed paddling in the pond and through the marsh, but a bit more challenge as you head north into Nantucket Sound and then return south to weave around the boats in Edgartown Harbor. For additional paddling, you can continue south through Edgartown's inner harbor to Katama Bay (Trip 34) or head east to Chappaquiddick and Cape Poge Bay (Trip 38).

Lighthouse Beach, which extends one mile from Eel Pond to Edgartown Harbor, offers opportunities for swimming, picnicking, bird-watching, shelling, and sun-bathing.

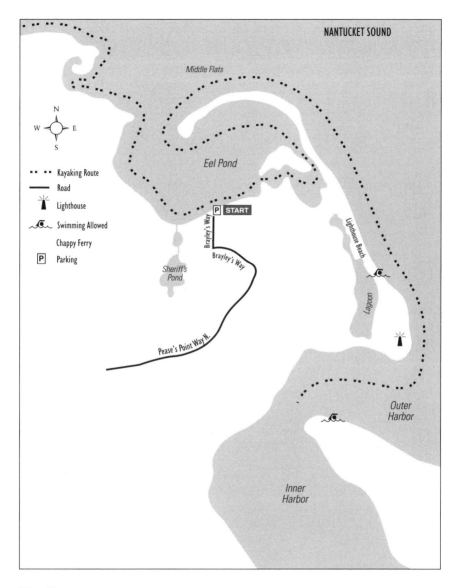

The Course

1. From the boat launch, turn left in a northerly direction, following the shore of Eel Pond. The undeveloped land behind the pond is Sheriff's Meadow Sanctuary (Trip 2).

Eel Pond ends at a marsh, a bird-watcher's delight. You may spot **American oystercatchers,** black and white birds that use their long, pointed red

Edgartown homes and boathouses as seen from Edgartown Harbor.

bills to pry open mollusks. Their competition may be small brown birds with skinny yellow legs and long pointed bills, named **lesser yellowlegs.**

2. Continue past the marsh, paddle around the rocks and make a sharp left turn to head into Nantucket Sound. This route skirts Cow Bay and ends at the three-mile-long John Sylvia State Beach on the north shore.

3. To return, head back into Eel Pond, passing your starting point to wind your way in and out of the salt marsh that lies behind Lighthouse Beach.

4. After exploring the marsh, go around the peninsula (watch for the sand bars) and follow the beach south as it heads toward Edgartown Lighthouse and the harbor. You may be accompanied by **least terns**, small white birds with black caps that dive head first into the water for fish.

The **Edgartown Lighthouse** sits at the entrance to Edgartown Harbor. The lighthouse originally was built on an artificial island of granite blocks that was connected to the mainland by a wooden walkway. When the walkway eroded, a causeway was built to replace it. Natural forces created a replacement for the causeway when water currents formed a small barrier beach, now named Lighthouse Beach.

5. If you decide to continue your trip south toward Katama Bay, carefully cross between the two ferry boats that continuously shuttle cars, bikes, and pedestrians between Edgartown and Chappaquiddick.

If you wish to swim, cross to the Chappaquiddick side of the harbor. A small beach, owned by the Martha's Vineyard Land Bank, lies just north of the On-Time Ferry Dock.

Following the long stretch of beach on Chappaquiddick's north shore will eventually lead to Cape Poge Bay.

TRIP 36
EDGARTOWN GREAT POND

Location: Edgartown

Rating: Easy to moderate. Windy conditions from the southwest often prevail on the open pond, especially from 2:30 to 5 P.M., but the sheltered coves offer protection. The pond is quite shallow and the coves, more so.

Distance: The pond is 1.5 miles long and 0.5 mile wide. The distance from the open pond to the tip of the longest cove, Wintucket, is approximately 2 miles.

With its convenient location and scenic, protected coves, Edgartown Great Pond is a great place to paddle.

Directions

From the intersection of Barnes Road and the Edgartown-West Tisbury Road, travel east 2.5 miles on the Edgartown-West Tisbury Road to Meeting House Way. Turn right and proceed 1.3 miles down this unpaved and very rutted road. Turn right onto another dirt road, distinguished by a grassy island between two entrances. Follow this road for 0.8 mile to the public landing. Drop off your boat at the end of the road and park around the circle.

Trip Description

At the end of a bumpy dirt road lies the public boat launch for Edgartown Great Pond, a wide body of water with one long cove and several shorter

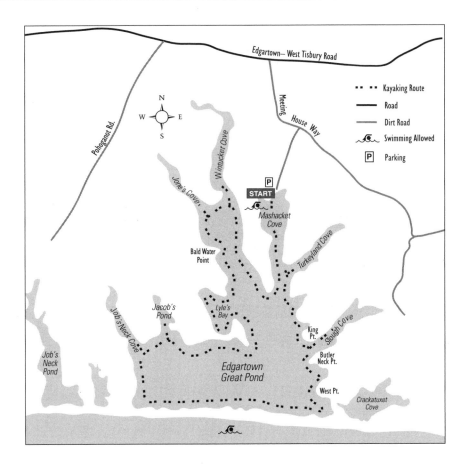

ones. You can spend a day exploring the whole pond or one hour paddling in one of the coves. Allow about two hours to visit Job's Neck and Jane's Cove. If you wish to explore the largest cove, Wintucket, allow two hours. Paddling from Meshacket to Slough and Turkeyland Coves on the east side takes approximately 1 1/2 hours.

Swimming is possible in the pond, off the small beach at the launching area or in the ocean, south of the barrier beach.

The Course

1. Begin at the public landing on Meshacket Cove. If you prefer get-away-from-it-all paddling, head for the west side of the pond. At the southeast edge lies Job's Neck Cove, an undeveloped inlet bordered by marsh grass.

2. Proceeding north from the cove, you will discover tiny Jacob's Pond tucked behind the grass. High tide may allow passage into the pond.

3. From the main pond, following the shore leads to Lyles Bay.

4. To visit my favorite, Jane's Cove, continue to follow the western shore.

Paddling to the tip of the cove reveals a landscape inhabited only by wildlife. Tall trees and decayed tree trunks provide perfect habitats for a variety of shorebirds. The last time I was there, I saw an **osprey** in a nest on its original habitat—a dead tree trunk, not the telephone poles that serve as substitute nesting platforms all over the island. A **great blue heron** flew away as I approached, leaving her brown youngster perched on a dead limb. The young heron was too busy looking around for its mother to notice me so I was able to get close enough to almost touch it until the young heron plunged into the water and paddled away.

5. When returning to Meshacket Cove, head south toward the barrier beach. Upon reaching the open pond across from the beach, head north. Meshacket Cove and the boat landing are directly across from the beach. The cove is distinguished by a gray-shingled house perched at the midpoint of its northern tip.

6. To see Wintucket Cove, proceed out of Meshacket Cove and turn right, passing Kanomika Neck on your right. Here you can forage for your lunch, as the southern tip of Kanomika Neck often is studded with clams.

7. The wide cove branches into two smaller ones, Jane's Cove on the left and the longer Wintucket Cove on the right. If you paddle to the tip of Wintucket Cove, you'll come to a weir, placed across the inlet to divert the water. While paddling in these narrow coves, stay in the middle to avoid the shallow coastline.

8. Two small coves lie east of Mashacket Cove. The first, Turkeyland Cove, is less developed than Slough Cove. Lined with older cottages, Slough Cove was the first to be developed. The other coves have fewer houses because each of these newer homes sits on at least 3 acres of land.

9. When returning from the east side of the pond, remember that Turkeyland and Meshacket Coves form a V, with the boat launch on the left side of the V.

TRIP 37
POUCHA POND

$ 🏊

Location: Chappaquiddick

Rating: Easy. The only hazard is trying to paddle while slapping the greenhead flies in July and the mosquitoes in August (bring along bug repellent).

Distance: The pond is 1.4 miles long and 0.5 mile wide at its widest point. Allow 1.5 to 2 hours to circle the pond.

Fees: Round trip fees for the Chappy Ferry are $12.00 for car and driver, $3.00 for each additional passenger, $6.00 for cyclists.

Relaxed paddling and great bird-watching in a small, shallow, sheltered pond make this an ideal trip for inexperienced paddlers.

Directions

Take the Chappy Ferry to Chappaquiddick. Travel 2.5 miles on Chappaquiddick Road. When the road bends sharply to the right, continue straight onto unpaved Dike Road. Follow Dike Road to the end at Dike Bridge and East Beach. Get there early, as parking is limited. Do not park along the road as you will be ticketed. If the lot is full, you can drop off your boat and park in the Mytoi parking lot, 0.2 mile back down Dike Road.

Trip Description

One can paddle in the open pond or weave in and out of the salt marsh, a favorite nesting and feeding spot for a variety of shorebirds, such as kingfishers, great blue herons, American oystercatchers, herring gulls, cormorants, and snowy egrets. Poucha Pond borders two conservation areas: Wasque Reservation and Poucha Pond Reservation. Wasque offers hiking trails, picnic benches and the opportunity to jump the waves on the south coast or swim off the calmer eastern shore.

The Trustees of Reservations, which manages East Beach, offers naturalist-led canoe and kayak tours and rentals from June to September. The rentals are for members only, but it is easy and relatively inexpensive to join.

More intrepid and energetic paddlers can extend their trip by heading into Cape Poge Bay (Trip 38).

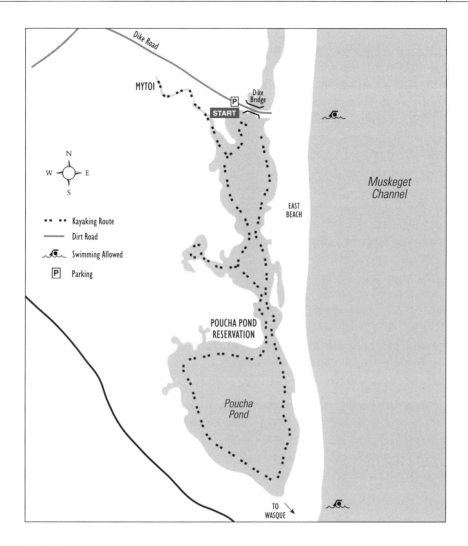

The Course

1. Put in your boat to the right of Dike Bridge, named for a dike constructed in the mid-1800s to control the flow of water into Poucha Pond.

During winter, the dike was closed to keep the water fresh. In spring, the gates of the dike were opened to allow herring and shad to swim into the pond and deposit their eggs in the protected waters.

2. Head south and stay to the right, following the marsh on the eastern shore. Turn right into the first inlet. You can paddle quite a way into this serene but smelly channel, passing the Marsh Trail through Mytoi on the right.

As you paddle amidst the marsh grass, you may notice shorebirds surveying the water for their next meal. You can't miss the **American oystercatcher**, which sports a long, bright orange bill, and a dark brown upper body with a white belly. It's also easy to spot the **great blue heron**, mostly light gray with a yellow bill and a long neck and legs.

Two different types of grasses grow in the marsh. Growing next to the water is a stiff spiky grass called **cordgrass**. The thinner-leaved grass that bends in the wind is called **salt marsh hay**, used by early settlers to feed their sheep and cattle. As you paddle in and out of the marsh, you'll notice thousands of **Atlantic ribbed mussels** attached to the roots of the grass.

The course passes by a peninsula, a section of Poucha Pond Reservation. Because the peninsula is surrounded by marsh, it is difficult to pull your boat ashore to explore. In this section you may discover remnants of the vegetation planted by the Poucha Pond Meadow and Fishing Company, Chappaquiddick landowners who built the dike. In the last 100 years, new growth has replaced the old, but the vegetation continues to attract water fowl, which was the purpose for the planting in the first place. Three varieties of herons feed in this area: the **short green heron**, the **great blue heron** and the **black-crowned night heron.** You may also spot **marsh hawks, egrets,** and **short-eared owls**.

3. Follow the shore until you reach the sandy southern tip.

A harbor was located here during pre-Colonial times. By 1722, storms, winds, and tides had filled in the opening to the sea. As a result, the salt water in the pond became fresh water.

In the 1800s, wild cranberries flourished at this end of the pond, and workers often harvested as many as four barrels a day.

4. You can pull your boat ashore at the southeast corner to visit Wasque Reservation, a Trustees of Reservations property with hiking trails, toilets, and a magnificent beach with pounding surf (Trip 6).

To head into the reservation, follow the path next to the fenced-in area (for the protection of terns and plovers) until you reach the water. You probably will find people fishing at Wasque Point, the junction of the south and east coasts. Swimming is not allowed here because of dangerous riptides. For big surf, turn right and swim along the south shore. For calmer water, turn left onto East Beach.

5. To return, follow the east coast north to Dike Bridge.

TRIP 38
CAPE POGE BAY

Location: Chappaquiddick

Rating: Moderate. Because the bay is quite exposed, be prepared for wind and chop.

Distance: 2.5 miles long, 1.2 miles wide. Allow 4 hours to paddle the perimeter of the entire pond.

Fees: Round trip fees for the Chappy Ferry are $12.00 for car and driver, $3.00 for each additional passenger, $6.00 for cyclists.

This pristine pond at the northern tip of Chappaquiddick offers the most remote paddling opportunity on the Vineyard.

Directions
Take the ferry to Chappaquiddick (again, early is best; in summer, long lines are possible from 10 A.M. to 1 P.M. and on the return from 4 P.M. to 6 P.M.) Travel 2.5 miles on Chappaquiddick Road. When the road bends sharply right, continue straight onto unpaved Dike Road. Follow Dike Road to the end at Dike Bridge and East Beach. You can park only on the west side of the lot. If the lot is full, go back down Dike Road 0.2 mile and park in the Mytoi lot.

Trip Description
At Cape Poge Bay, your only companions in this undeveloped "almost pond" (a narrow channel is the only opening to Nantucket Sound) may be seagulls and the occasional person fishing for scallops. There are plenty of terrific places to swim and sun as the tour begins at East Beach and travels beside a 2.5-mile-long barrier beach in Cape Poge Wildlife Refuge. Paddling around the bay entitles you to explore the refuge where you'll also find sand dunes, salt marsh and tidal flats. Among the birds that nest and feed here are osprey, oystercatchers, piping plovers, and least and common terns. Arrive early at East Beach. Parking is limited.

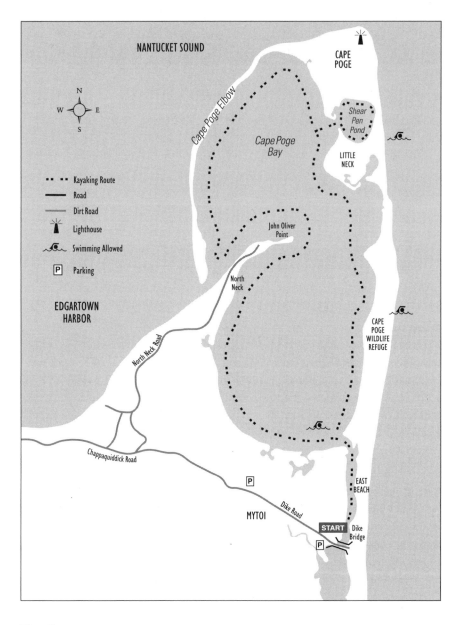

The Course

1. Launch your boat on the north (left) side of Dike Bridge. Hug the east shore as you paddle north through the lagoon toward Cape Poge Bay. Proceed toward the sandy beach straight ahead. Upon arrival at the beach, you

Discovering Cape Poge Bay.

will see the opening into Cape Poge Bay. If you want to stop and swim in warm calm water, this protected spot, just before the bay, is a good choice.

2. Once in the bay, continue north, following the coastline. On the east side you'll see the three-mile barrier beach of Cape Poge Wildlife Refuge. East of the refuge lies the Muskeget Channel in Nantucket Sound.

In the shallow water, you may spot a strange, dark form scuttling under the sand searching for soft-shelled clams. This large sea animal, known as a **horseshoe**, or **king crab,** is related to the scorpion and has been around since prehistoric times. Its long sharp tail at the end of its shell lowers for digging and rises to defend.

In the middle of the pond, where the water is deeper, you'll paddle over jungles of eel grass, home to fin and shellfish that, in turn, attract shorebirds.

Plan on paddling for an hour before arriving at a small peninsula, defined by an osprey pole, followed by a round inlet, called Shear Pen Pond. Its name refers to its use three hundred years ago when sheep were herded here to be washed and then shorn of their wool.

At the northeastern tip of the barrier beach sits Cape Poge Lighthouse, which has welcomed ships sailing to Edgartown Harbor since 1802. The current lighthouse, built in 1893, replaced earlier ones that were destroyed by winds and/or beach erosion. Because the light stands 63 feet high, it signals ships as far as 9 miles away.

You'll notice that this section at the northernmost point of Cape Poge is more fertile than the barren eastern strip. Because the terrain here is so different from the rest of the barrier beach, some people believe it once was a separate island, now linked by the eventual build-up of sand caused by winds and ocean currents. Some historians believe this linkage could have occurred as early as the thirteenth century while others are of the opinion that it remained an island until the early 1700s.

3. Continue around the tip of the bay, now heading south, to paddle next to Cape Poge Elbow, a slender strip of land, inhabited by **herring** and **black-backed gulls**.

These gulls subsist mainly on shellfish. To break open the hard crustaceans, the gulls fly into the air with their victims in their beaks and then fling them onto hard ground. If you visit in June, the Elbow will be replete with gull eggs and the protective mothers will dive bomb if you venture too close to the nests.

4. Cape Poge Elbow ends at Cape Poge Gut, a narrow opening with a swift current that leads to Edgartown Harbor and Nantucket Sound. At this point head east to skirt North Neck and then pass by the more developed northern side of Chappaquiddick.

5. Upon reaching the eastern side of Chappaquiddick, turn right or south to return via the lagoon to Dike Bridge.

TRIP 39
SENGEKONTACKET AND TRAPP'S PONDS

Location: Oak Bluffs and Edgartown

Rating: Easy to moderate, depending on the wind. If paddling in summer with the wind out of the southwest, explore in the morning and early afternoon as the wind increases later in the day.

Distance: 2.5 miles long and 0.5 mile wide. It takes 3 to 4 hours to paddle around the entire pond.

You will find visual variety with many opportunities to stop and explore.

Directions

The public boat ramp is located on the south side of Beach Road, 1.8 miles from Oak Bluffs Terminal and 3.2 miles from the intersection with the Edgartown-Vineyard Haven Road in Edgartown. Look for Andy's Frozen Lemonade stand, which often sits in the parking area. You can park in the lot or along Beach Road.

Trip Description

Sengekontacket, an American Indian name meaning "at the bursting forth of the tidal stream," lies next to Joseph Sylvia State Beach. And Sengekontacket Pond "bursts forth" with much to see and do. You can pull up your boat and stroll along the trails and view waterfowl at Felix Neck Wildlife Sanctuary, Pecoy Point Preserve and Caroline Tuthill Preserve; stop at several deserted islands; swim in the pond or the ocean; sneak a closer look at golfers teeing off at Farm Neck Golf Course and searching the water for mishit balls; weave your way through an inlet that leads to a salt marsh at the end of Majors Cove; and portage across Beach Road to explore Trapp's Pond.

The Course

1. From the boat launching area, head right (north) to swing by Farm Neck, the most scenic and popular golf course on the island. Luxurious homes border the links, including one that belongs to film director Spike Lee.

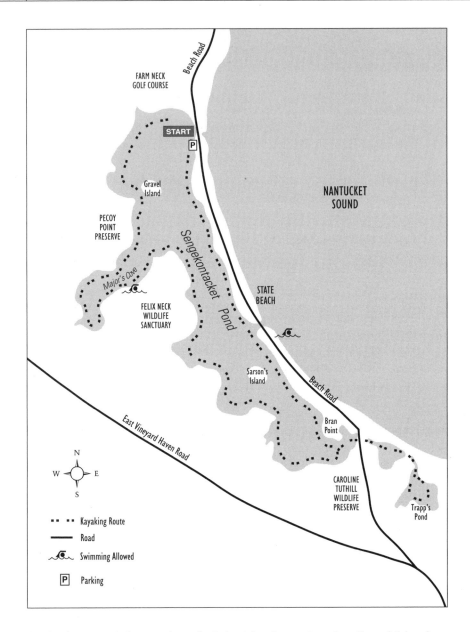

2. Circle around the north end of the island, passing tiny Gravel Island on the left and a development, also named Sengekontacket, on the right.

The Martha's Vineyard Land Bank has used a 2 percent fee tacked onto real estate purchases to acquire **Pecoy Point Preserve**, ahead on the right.

If you wish to explore the preserve, you can secure your boat at the boat slide.

3. A right turn into an inlet named Major's Cove affords a glimpse on the left of **Felix Neck Wildlife Sanctuary**, owned by the Massachusetts Audubon Society. If the tide is high, hug the right side of the cove and paddle through a narrow channel into a scenic salt marsh, often frequented by mallards, geese, swans, great blue herons, and osprey.

4. Return from the cove to the pond by paddling on the right or south side to have a bird's eye view of Felix Neck. Ahead on the right is a small sandy beach where you can pull up your boat if you wish to explore the property (Trip 4).

5. Returning from Major's Cove to the open pond, bend right to follow the shoreline. The center of the pond around Sarson's Island, on your left, is quite shallow.

Sarson's Island, owned by Felix Neck Wildlife Sanctuary, is often covered with hundreds of black birds with outstretched wings, long necks and hooked beaks, named **double-crested cormorants**. While searching for the pounds of fish they consume each day, the cormorants skim the pond, their wings often catching water with each flap. Because their bodies don't produce enough oil to easily shed water, as is the case for ducks, geese, and swans, cormorants stop frequently to open their wings to dry them. See if you can see one taking off; the wings are quite heavy and force the cormorants to first drop to the water before gaining altitude.

6. Bear right into the bay, passing another salt marsh, a favorite nesting and feeding place for waterfowl. Look for brightly colored **wood ducks** swimming amid the grass.

Cormorant

Wood duck

Paddling under the bridge to Trapp's Pond.

7. As you continue toward the east end of the pond, you'll notice that the coast becomes more densely populated. Older homes on the Vineyard did not have the conservation codes that now require that dwellings be built at least 100 feet from the water.

The wooded area at the northeastern tip is the **Caroline Tuthill Wildlife Preserve** (Trip 3), a property owned by another conservation organization, Sheriff's Meadow. If you wish to stretch your legs and pick some blueberries while taking a pleasant 1.3-mile walk, pull up your boat at the clearing and refer to Trip 3.

8. Continue around the east end of the pond, past the tiny peninsula named Bran Point: You may spot adults and children armed with nets gathering crabs from Menada Creek.

9. At the northeast end of the pond, a small sandy spot often flanked by moored boats is the best place to access **Trapp's Pond**. Pull up your kayak and portage it across Beach Road to the boat landing for Trapp's Pond. From there you can explore this tranquil spot. Trapp's Pond is divided into two bodies of water: the first is bounded by a barrier beach to Nantucket sound where small beach shacks dot the dunes.

10. To pass to the second body of water, paddle under a tiny bridge.

This pond is bordered on the east side by Edgartown Golf Club, a private nine-hole course. Most homes are set back from the water and are hidden by shrubbery so you have a sense of complete isolation, except for a single great blue heron, an osprey, or a pair of swans.

11. Return by the same route, portage and put the kayak back into Sengekontacket Pond.

12. The return skirts the southeast shore, where you can pull up your boat and stop for a swim, either in the shallow pond or in the ocean. As you paddle the remaining 2 miles back to your starting point, you can watch cyclists, in-line skaters, and joggers on the Beach Road bike path, the most popular one on the island.

TRIP 40
LAGOON POND

Location: Oak Bluffs and Tisbury

Rating: Easy to Moderate: Lagoon Pond sits in a protected location so there usually is neither much wind nor current, but boats entering and exiting do create wakes.

Distance: 2 miles long and 0.4 mile wide. Allow a couple of hours to tour the pond.

At this centrally located pond, you will find easy access and kayak and canoe rentals nearby.

Directions
The state boat launch is on Beach Road in Vineyard Haven, 0.6 mile east of the Steamship Authority Terminal and 0.2 mile west of the drawbridge.

Trip Description
If you are looking for a central location to launch your boat or just want a boat to launch, Lagoon Pond is for you. Separated from Vineyard Haven Harbor by a causeway and drawbridge, this deep pond serves as refuge for boats during major storms. Small pleasure craft are moored in the pond and often line

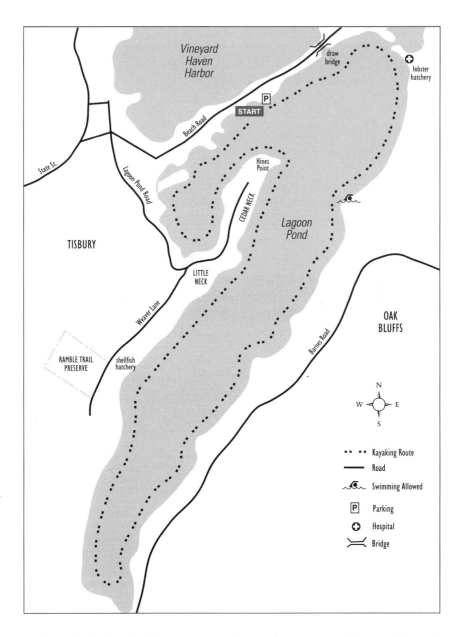

up behind the drawbridge—it opens frequently—to enter Vineyard Sound. You also can choose to head into the harbor, but don't bother waiting for the bridge to open; you can paddle under it. If you want to escape motorboats, paddle into the cove on the western side of the lagoon or proceed down the southern tip. Try to avoid weekends, when boat traffic is the heaviest.

Half of Lagoon Pond is in the town of Tisbury; the other half is in Oak Bluffs. The tour follows the Tisbury shore and returns on the Oak Bluffs side.

Winds Up, located about 500 feet from the public boat launch, provides rentals (and lessons too). Other options include exploring the Ramble Trail Preserve, stopping at the State Lobster Hatchery for a tour, or swimming at a public beach in the pond.

The Course

1. From the launch site, head west, following the northern shore. Windsurfers, kayakers, and sailors cluster around Winds Up, a store that rents and sells boats.

2. Proceed into the cove, lined with businesses and boatyards, but no boat traffic (too shallow). Circle around a peninsula named Hines Point. Be careful not to run aground in this shallow section.

3. For more tranquil paddling, head down the western Tisbury side toward the southern tip of the pond.

At the halfway point along the western coast, you will enter a small bay. Watch for rectangular containers in the water near the shore. These containers belong to the **Shellfish Hatchery** and are used to propagate shellfish. Lagoon Pond is seeded for scallops and you may spot people digging for the succulent mollusks. In front of the hatchery rest a number of "boxes" used for scallop propagation.

South of the Shellfish Hatchery lies the **Ramble Trail Preserve**, a small property owned by the Martha's Vineyard Land Bank. To identify the property, look for a number of boats lying on the beach. Behind the boats, stairs lead to the trails. You can hike to the top of the bluff for an overview of Lagoon Pond and stroll along the Ramble Trail, one of the first paths constructed on the island for recreational walking.

Shore birds frequent this more remote section. Black **cormorants** dry their wings on rafts and docks, colorful **mallards** paddle by and **herring gulls** search for supper.

4. After circling around the tip and heading north (often helped by a tailwind), you leave the Tisbury side of the pond and enter Oak Bluffs.

About halfway up, you'll notice a sandy strip, often inhabited by sunbathers and swimmers. The southern half belongs to landowners but the northern section is public. Feel free to stop and swim.

Further up the coast, a silo marks the site of the State Lobster Hatchery. Here researchers study the living habits of lobsters. The Martha's Vineyard Hospital sits next to the hatchery.

5. If you wish to enter Vineyard Haven Harbor, paddle under the drawbridge. Be alert for boats entering and exiting.

6. To return to the boat launch, pass the bridge and continue paddling west.

TRIP 41
LAKE TASHMOO

Location: Tisbury

Rating: Easy: Because Tashmoo is small and sheltered, wind and chop seldom present a problem. But you will have to contend with boat traffic and current in the channel.

Check the tide schedule, as the northeast side of the lake can become quite shallow during low tide.

Distance: 1.4 miles long, 0.6 miles at its widest point. You can circumnavigate the lake in 90 minutes.

This small, scenic lake is a good choice if you want a short excursion and/or a swim in Vineyard Sound.

Directions
From State Road in Tisbury, go north on West Spring Street (just east of the Tashmoo Overlook). Bear left at the stop sign. Take the second left onto Pine Street. At the stop sign, turn left onto Lake Street. Follow Lake until it ends at the Tisbury Town Landing. You can park for 4 hours in the lot on the south side of the road.

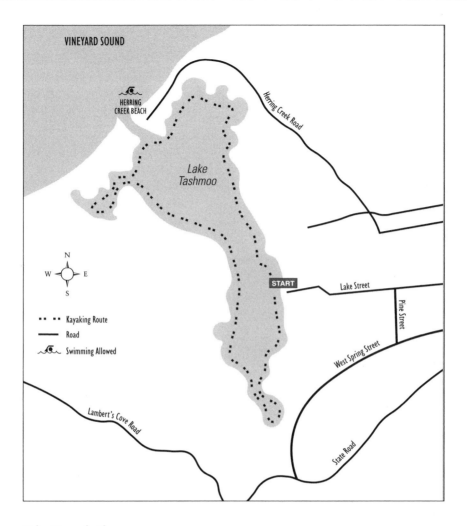

Trip Description

For a preview of coming attractions, stop at the Lake Tashmoo Overlook on State Road in Vineyard Haven to watch boats motoring in and out of Vineyard Sound. From this picture-postcard setting, it's a five-minute drive to this small picturesque lake. My favorite areas are the quiet coves on the southern and northwestern tips.

The Course

1. From the dock, head north, and paddle around the sail, fishing and motor boats moored in this small harbor. Follow the shoreline while staying away from the channel, which runs down the middle of the lake, where fighting the current and dodging boat traffic can alter your course.

2. Follow the coast as it bends east. This section can be quite shallow, so you may get exercise from pulling your boat rather than paddling. Herring Creek Beach is located on the northeast side of the lake. Here you can swim at the lifeguard supervised beach on the Sound, relax on the sand or wade in the lake.

3. To cross to the west side of the lake, carefully traverse the channel and watch for boats entering from Vineyard Sound.

Perched on the northwest corner of the outlet to the ocean sits an imposing residence, named Chip Chop, former home of actress Katherine Cornell and now owned by television commentator Diane Sawyer and director Mike Nichols.

4. Head west into the calm cove and then go all the way down to the southern tip to explore the less developed section of the lake. Here the only traffic consists of ducks and geese paddling about.

TRIP 42
TISBURY GREAT POND

Location: West Tisbury

Rating: Moderate: On windy days, or after 2:30 P.M. when the wind increases, you may have difficulty paddling southwest against the wind on the open pond and will find easier paddling in the sheltered coves.

Distance: The pond itself is about 1 mile long and a half-mile wide. The coves range from 0.5 to 2 miles long. You can spend an hour or two paddling in and out of the coves or a whole day exploring the entire pond.

Restrooms: A portable toilet is located at the parking area east of the boat launch onto Tisbury Great Pond.

As you explore this body of water you will find that it resembles a hand, with each finger a cove and the thumb Black Point Pond.

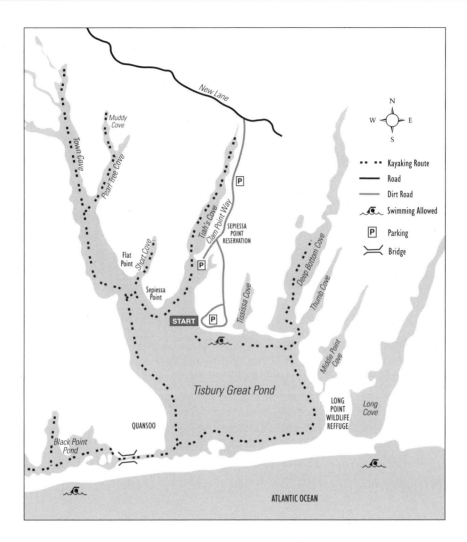

Directions

The boat launch site is at Sepiessa Point Reservation. To reach the reservation, proceed 3 miles west of the entrance to the Martha's Vineyard Airport on the Edgartown-West Tisbury Road. Turn left onto New Lane. Follow New Lane for 1.2 miles. Turn right onto Clam Point Way, a dirt road that leads to the reservation. Continue on the road about 500 feet past the first parking area to the second parking lot. It's a short walk to haul your boat into Tiah's Cove. If you prefer to spend more time driving than paddling, proceed one mile to the end of the dirt road and unload your boat at the launch area.

An anchor on the shore of Tisbury Great Pond.

Trip Description

A wide variety of visual delights await you as you discover the many inlets and coves in Tisbury Great Pond. Make sure to leave time for a visit to Black Point Pond.

Do wear foot covering to protect against the sharp shells and the pincers of the blue-claw crab. If you bring along a bucket and net, you can attempt to catch the elusive crabs that emerge in late afternoon.

Picnicking, hiking, and swimming are offered at Sepiessa Point Reservation and Long Point Reservation.

The Course

The water level in Tisbury Great Pond fluctuates greatly, depending on when the pond has been opened to the sea. Workers cut a breach through the barrier beach when the pond reaches a certain height so the resident oysters will have the salt water they need to breed.

1. Paddle out Tiah's Cove to Tisbury Great Pond. Head right to explore the longest finger, Town Cove. Allow an hour and a half for a leisurely investigation of this undeveloped section, consisting mainly of farmland. The first inlet on the right is Short Cove, followed by Pear Tree Cove, which branches into Muddy Cove.

2. From Town Cove, head south toward the barrier beach. The narrow channel to Black Point Pond remains hidden until you reach the barrier beach.

3. To visit this tranquil pond, turn right down the channel. Unless the water level is low, you should have no trouble paddling beside the marsh grass. Make sure you duck your head when passing under the bridge to the pond.

Navigating the channel is worth the effort as you are likely to be the only non-waterfowl inhabitant of this undeveloped spot. You can explore its coves, stop for a swim in the pond or follow the path through the marsh grass to the ocean while admiring the **great blue herons** that frequent the pond.

4. From Black Point Pond, you can return by following the barrier beach east toward Long Point Wildlife Refuge. Shallow water in Tisbury Great Pond indicates that the pond recently has been opened to the ocean. Look at the west side of the barrier beach for a narrow channel running out to the sea (often filled with children riding the current).

5. Continue past the barrier beach, following the coast as it turns north.

Long Point Reservation, a Trustees of Reservations property described in Trip 11, lies on your right. If you wish to stop for a swim or hike its trails, pull your boat onto the beach. Stairs ascend from the shore to a path. If you go right, you'll discover a glorious beach. A left turn leads to hiking trails.

6. Proceeding around the pond to Middle Point Cove, you'll discover that this cove has not yet actually reached cove status. However, it's just a matter of time before the land separating this pond will be washed away and it actually will become a cove.

7. Next, on the right, are the "two for the price of one" coves. As you head into Thumb Cove, you'll notice that it forks, revealing Deep Bottom Cove as well. Allow an hour to explore these two coves.

8. The last cove is Tississa Cove, which flanks the east side of Sepiessa Point Reservation (Trip 12).

If you wish to end your trip with a swim or a hike through the reservation, pass Tississa Cove and pull your boat up onto the sand. If you have parked near the boat launch at Tiah's Cove, you have the option of following the Red Trail one mile through the reservation to your car and then driving back to pick up your boat.

9. Returning on the open pond from the barrier beach or Black Point Pond to Tiah's Cove can be tricky. My trusty locators are the red barn on the west side of Tisisissa Cove, the orange steps on the beach at Sepiessa Point to the right of the boat launch, and the osprey pole next to the boat launch at the southern end of Tiah's Cove.

TRIP 43
CHILMARK POND

Location: Chilmark

Rating: Easy to moderate: Relaxed paddling unless there is a strong southwest wind. Doctor's Creek requires perseverance and some skillful paddling.

Distance: 2 miles long and 0.25 mile wide. Allow several hours to explore both the upper and lower ponds.

One of the smallest bodies of water in this guide, Chilmark Pond compensates for its size by offering variety, tranquility, beauty, and many species of shorebirds.

Directions

From the intersection of the Edgartown/West Tisbury Road and South Road in the town of West Tisbury, head west 3.2 miles. It's easy to miss the tiny Land Bank sign on the crest of the hill on the left side. Turn left and follow the road to the small parking lot. Get there early to guarantee a spot. (There is room for only 10 cars.)

Trip Description

A narrow cove in Chilmark Lower Pond leads to Doctor's Creek, which snakes its way through dense marsh grass to Chilmark Upper Pond, where yet another cove awaits exploration. Swimming is nearby at a Martha's Vineyard Land Bank-owned section of spectacular Hancock Beach.

The depth of this freshwater pond varies depending on when an opening has been cut in the barrier beach. If you visit in May or early June, right after the opening of the pond to the ocean, you will find a much shallower pond than in late summer.

The Course

1. After launching your boat, head left into a small cove. Proceed east to a longer narrower inlet, Wade's Cove, at the northeast tip of the pond.

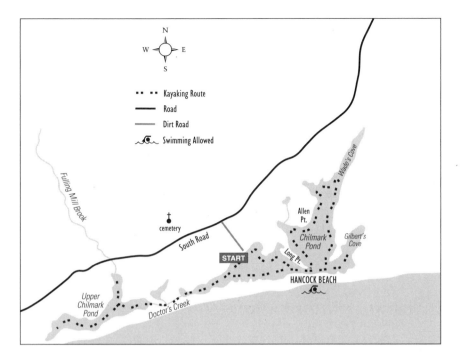

Shorebirds often congregate around the marsh grass. The last time I visited, I spotted a great blue heron, swans, double-crested cormorants, mottled ducks, Canada geese, herring gulls, and common terns.

2. Continue paddling up the east side of the pond to head into Gilbert's Cove. This section tends to be shallow so you may not get too far.

If you are interested in sunning and swimming at the Land Bank beach, head west about a quarter-mile. Look for two orange flags that mark the Land Bank boundaries. A boardwalk and stairs lead from the pond to the beach. The public could not access this private beach until 1993, when the Martha's Vineyard Land Bank purchased 8.3 acres of land that adjoined the pond and a portion of private beach. The Land Bank then constructed an access road, small parking lot, and boat launching area.

3. From the beach, continue west to Doctor's Creek, the narrow grassy connector to Chilmark Upper Pond.

If you enter, be advised that at times you will be convinced that the phragmites have taken over and there is no outlet to the next pond. But persevere and you will emerge. The return will be much easier because the current and southwest wind will push you along. Your paddling companions may be blue-claw crabs that skitter along the creek floor.

4. Now in Upper Pond, look to the west at the colorful cliffs of Lucy Vincent Beach. Paddle north to explore Warren Tilton Cove where the Fulling Mill Brook ends.

5. Loop around the pond and head back along the south shore to return through Doctor's Creek to Lower Pond.

TRIP 44
MENEMSHA, NASHAQUITSA, AND STONEWALL PONDS

Location: Chilmark

Rating: Easy to moderate: Stonewall and Nashaquitsa Ponds are protected and usually calm. Windy conditions often exist on Menemsha Pond.

Distance: 2 miles long, 1 mile wide. Allow 30 minutes for Stonewall Pond and an hour for each of the other ponds. To paddle from coast to coast, allow 3 to 4 hours.

Take this trip to paddle from the south shore of Martha's Vineyard to the north coast.

Directions
The boat launch for Nashaquitsa Pond is located on South Road, 1.3 miles west of Beetlebung Corner (the intersection of South Road, Middle Road, and Menemsha Cross Road in Chilmark Center). The small parking lot is on the right side of the road, just past a small bridge. If you get to the Nashaquitsa Pond Overlook, you've gone too far. If the lot is filled, there is limited parking on the side of the road, but be careful as you will get ticketed if any of your tires are on the pavement or if there is a No Parking sign in the vicinity.

Trip Description
At the narrow western end of Martha's Vineyard, you can paddle across the island from the Atlantic Ocean to Vineyard Sound. The course begins at Stonewall Pond and runs under South Road to Nashaquitsa Pond, which flows into Menemsha Pond on the north side of the island. Swimming is

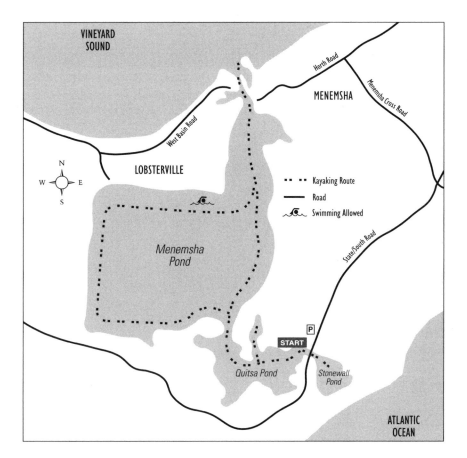

permitted at stony Stonewall Beach on the south, Lobsterville Beach on the northeast side of Menemsha Pond, and Menemsha Beach on Vineyard Sound.

Each of these bodies of water has its own character. Stonewall Pond is small, sheltered, and often filled with shorebirds. Nashaquitsa Pond appears as a small, protected harbor with several long coves. Menemsha Pond is quite the opposite—open, often windy, the perfect location for weekly regattas.

The Course

1. From the boat launch at Nashaquitsa (known locally as Quitsa) Pond, turn right to paddle under the bridge to Stonewall Pond.

Canada geese and **mallards** often swim in this tiny pond.

Menemsha Harbor

2. Proceed straight across the pond to reach the path to Stonewall Beach. If you follow the path you'll discover why the pond and beach are named "Stonewall."

3. Upon your return to Quitsa Pond, paddle to the right if you are interested in exploring quiet coves, with nothing but dragonflies for company. As you head from one cove to the next, you will pass a large boulder resting in the middle of the pond, a favorite spot for **cormorants** to dry their wings.

4. Go straight to proceed into Menemsha Pond. Be prepared for some chop and wind. It's best to visit during the week so you won't have to dodge sailboats.

If you wish to sunbathe and swim, paddle to the sandy beach on the northeast side of the pond. Further west along the beach, the water is too shallow for swimming. Here you are likely to spot **least terns** swooping down to the water in their continual search for fish.

5. If you stay to the right of Menemsha Pond, you'll enter Menemsha Basin, a busy passageway for boats entering and exiting from Vineyard Sound.

The bike ferry shuttles bikes and their owners across the Basin to Lobsterville. One hundred years ago, the now deserted Lobsterville was the premier fishing village on the island. The dredging of the channel and creation of Menemsha Harbor caused Lobsterville to fall into disuse.

6. To reach Menemsha Beach you will have to fight the strong current in the channel and then turn right.

This beach is famous for its sunsets, when throngs picnic on the beach and applaud when the sun goes down.

7. To return, you can skirt the perimeter of Menemsha Pond or head straight back. To find the launching ramp, keep your eyes out for the little bridge located to the left of the ramp.

TRIP 45
SQUIBNOCKET POND

Location: Chilmark

Rating: Moderate: Much of the pond is open so wind and chop are the norm.

Distance: 1.2 miles long and 1.8 miles wide. Allow two hours to circle the pond.

This bucolic pond is one of the most scenic on Martha's Vineyard.

Directions
From Beetlebung Corner in Chilmark Center, travel west 2.1 miles. Turn left onto Squibnocket Road (no street sign), the first paved road on left. Follow to the parking lot at the end of the road.

Trip Summary
Sand dunes, rocky outcroppings, and small forested islands contribute to the rarified experience of paddling around Squibnocket Pond. Located on the west end of the island, Squibnocket is easy to find. *Unfortunately, visitors who are not residents of Aquinnah or Chilmark can park in the lot only after 5 P.M. during July and August.* Parking is permitted before 5 P.M. during the remainder of the year.

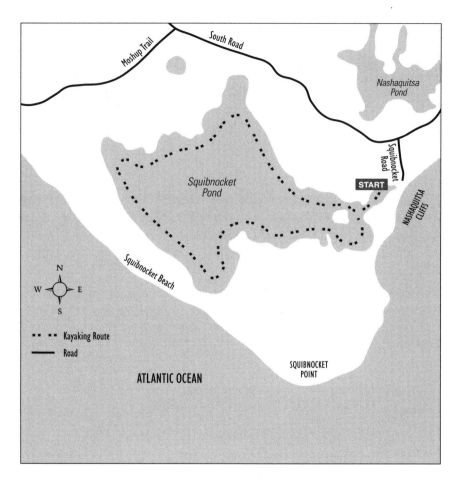

Trip Description

1. The exploration begins in an inlet where you will have to navigate through marsh grass, as this section is slowly reverting to swamp.

2. Once out of the inlet, head left to visit a saltmarsh with calm waters and a variety of shorebirds.

3. To reach the open pond, continue straight. I suggest bearing right of the island and following the shore, but not too closely, due to rocky outcroppings. As you proceed north and then west, you'll find the pond slowly revealing itself. You'll think you have reached the furthest point and then, suddenly you'll see another bay.

The large two-story gray-shingled home with several additions spread over many acres belonged to Jackie Kennedy Onassis and is now owned by her daughter Caroline.

4. Paddle toward the sand dunes on the west side of the pond where you will hear the sound of the surf pounding against the shore of an exquisite beach that, sadly, is restricted to residents.

Another sound may be the loud *whr-r-r* of swans taking off, if you come too close to them. During my last visit I witnessed a convention of swans slowly paddling across the pond and hundreds of cormorants sunning themselves on the rocks.

5. To find your way back to the inlet, look for the small island, paddle past it and follow the north shore in an easterly direction.

Appendix: Resources

Emergency
Ambulance, Fire, Police. 911
Martha's Vineyard Hospital, Linton Lane, Oak Bluffs. 508-693-0410

Bicycle Shops

VINEYARD HAVEN
Cycleworks, 351 State Road, 508-693-6966. Offers rentals, sales, and repairs.

Craig's Bicycles, 344 State Road, 508-693-8693. Offers rentals, sales, and repairs.

Martha's Bicycle Rental, 4 Lagoon Pond Road, 508-693-0782. Offers rentals.

OAK BLUFFS
Anderson's Bike Rentals, Circuit Avenue Ext., 508-693-9346. Offers rentals, sales, and repairs.

Ride On Mopeds & Bikes, 9 Oak Bluffs Avenue, 508-693-2076. Offers rentals.

Sun & Fun, 26 Lake Avenue, 508-693-5457. Offers rentals.

EDGARTOWN
R.W. Cutler Edgartown Bike Rentals. 1 Main Street/Triangle, 508-627-4052. www.marthasvineyardbikerentals.com. Offers rentals.

Edgartown Bicycles, 190 Upper Main Street, 508-627-9008. www.edgartownbicycle.com. Offers rentals, sales, and repairs.

Wheel Happy, 8 South Water Street, 508-627-5928, Upper Main St., 508-627-5881. Offers rentals, sales, and repairs.

Kayak Rental

VINEYARD HAVEN

Island Spirit Kayak, PO Box 1666, 508-693-9727. www.islandsspirit.com. Offers rentals and tours.

Island Water Sports, 100 Lagoon Pond Road, 508-693-7767. www.boatmv.us. Offers rentals.

Wind's Up, 199 Beach Road, 508-693-4252. www.windsupmv.com. Offers rentals, sales, instruction.

AQUINNAH

Book-A-Boat, 3 Church Street, 508-645-2400. Offers rentals and delivery.

Automobile Parking Areas for Bikers

VINEYARD HAVEN

Tisbury School, between Spring and William Streets (when school is not in session).

OAK BLUFFS

Martha's Vineyard Regional High School, Edgartown-Vineyard Haven Road (when school is not in session).

EDGARTOWN

Bike path entrances to the State Forest: two parking areas on the west side of Barnes (Airport) Road, 0.5 mile and 1.3 miles south of the Edgartown-Vineyard Haven Road intersection.

Edgartown-West Tisbury Road, across from Pohoganot Road, 1.6 miles east of Airport Rd.

State Forest: east side of Barnes Road, 0.8 mile south of the intersection with Edgartown-Vineyard Haven Road

Trolley shuttle lot: Dark Woods Road, off Edgartown-Vineyard Haven Road, east of the Triangle.

WEST TISBURY

Bike path entrances to the State Forest: Old County Road, one mile south of the State Road intersection.

Edgartown-West Tisbury Road, 1.6 miles west of the airport entrance road and across from Pond Rd.

Index

About the Author

LEE SINAI, a Massachusetts resident, is also the author of *Exploring in and around Boston on Bike and Foot*. When Lee is not writing, she prefers to be outdoors hiking, biking, kayaking, skiing, and playing tennis and golf.

Before becoming an author, Lee's previous careers included college administrator, tennis professional, and elementary school teacher. She received her undergraduate degree from the University of Michigan and a master's degree from Northwestern University.

The Appalachian Mountain Club

Founded in 1876, the AMC is the nation's oldest outdoor recreation and conservation organization. The AMC promotes the protection, enjoyment, and wise use of the mountains, rivers, and trails of the Northeast outdoors.

People
We are nearly 90,000 members in 12 chapters, 16,000 volunteers, and over 450 full-time and seasonal staff. Our chapters reach from Maine to Washington, D.C.

Outdoor Adventure and Fun
We offer more than 8,000 trips each year, from local chapter activities to major excursions worldwide, for every ability level and outdoor interest—from hiking and climbing to paddling, snowshoeing, and skiing.

Great Places to Stay
We host more than 150,000 guest nights each year at our AMC Lodges, Huts, Camps, Shelters, and Campgrounds. Each AMC Destination is a model for environmental education and stewardship.

Opportunities for Learning
We teach people the skills to be safe outdoors and to care for the natural world around us through programs for children, teens, and adults, as well as outdoor leadership training.

Caring for Trails
We maintain more than 1,700 miles of trails throughout the Northeast, including nearly 350 miles of the Appalachian Trail in five states.

Protecting Wild Places
We advocate for land and riverway conservation, monitor air quality, and work to protect alpine and forest ecosystems throughout the Northern Forest and Highlands regions.

Engaging the Public
We seek to educate and inform our own members and an additional 2 million people annually through AMC Books, our website, our White Mountain visitor centers, and AMC Destinations.

Join Us!
Members support our mission while enjoying great AMC programs, our award-winning *AMC Outdoors* magazine, and special discounts. Visit www.outdoors.org or call 617-523-0636 for more information.

THE APPALACHIAN MOUNTAIN CLUB
Recreation • Education • Conservation
www.outdoors.org

About the AMC Southeastern Massachusetts Chapter

The Appalachian Mountain Club's Southeastern Massachusetts Chapter offers outdoor activities, conducts trail work, and addresses local conservation issues south of Boston and on Cape Cod and the Islands. Programs range from hiking and cycling to skiing, paddling, and backpacking.

To view a list of AMC activities in Southeastern Massachusetts and other parts of the Northeast, visit: trips.outdoors.org

AMC Book Updates

AMC Books strives to keep our guidebooks as up-to-date as possible to help you plan safe and enjoyable adventures. If after publishing a book we learn that trails are relocated or route or contact information has changed, we will post the updated information online. Before you hit the trail, check for updates at www.outdoors.org/publications/books/updates.

While hiking or paddling, if you notice discrepancies with the trail description or map, or if you find any other errors in the book, please let us know by submitting them to amcbookupdates@outdoors.org or in writing to Books Editor, c/o AMC, 5 Joy Street, Boston, MA 02108. We will verify all submissions and post key updates each month.

AMC Books is dedicated to being a recognized leader in outdoor publishing. Thank you for your participation.

AMC BOOKS & MAPS

EXPLORE THE POSSIBILITIES

More Books from the Outdoor Experts

Massachusetts Trail Guide, 9th Edition

EDITED BY JOHN S. BURK

This revised and updated edition provides detailed descriptions of more than 400 trails across the state, including 70 new entries. Find your way easily and accurately with brand–new GPS rendered maps of the state's most popular areas–including the Blue Hills, Mount Wachusett, and Mount Greylock.

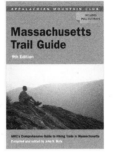

ISBN: 978-1-934028-25-4
$24.95

AMC'S Best Day Hikes Near Boston

BY MICHAEL TOUGIAS

This guide includes directions, trail maps, photos, and nature notes that highlight the natural history of the area. You'll also find out which trails are best for snowshoeing and cross-country skiing, making this guide an essential four-season reference.

ISBN: 978-1-929173-66-2
$16.95

Discover Cape Cod

BY MICHAEL O'CONNOR

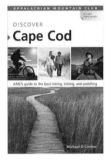

This book details 50 of the best hiking, biking, and paddling trips in this beautiful coastal area, including many excursions within the Cape Cod National Seashore. Nature notes and historical sidebars give visitors a more detailed picture of the area. For short, one–hour excursions or weekend afternoons, this guide provides the best outdoor experiences for vacationers and Cape Cod residents alike.

ISBN: 978-1-934028-17-9
$18.95

River Guide: Massachusetts, Connecticut, Rhode Island, 4th Edition

EDITED BY JOHN FISKE

In this completely updated and revised edition paddlers of all ability levels will find the information they need to experience waterways from serene rivers to challenging whitewater. In-depth river descriptions, a reader-friendly format, and detailed maps make trip planning quick and easy.

ISBN: 978-1-929173-87-7
$16.95

AMC BOOKS & MAPS
EXPLORE THE POSSIBILITIES

AMC Books & Maps: Explore the Possibilities

Shop online at www.outdoors.org/amcstore or call 800-262-4455
Appalachian Mountain Club • 5 Joy Street • Boston, MA 02108